Perfect Pitch

A Play

John Godber

A SAMUEL FRENCH ACTING EDITION

SAMUEL FRENCH

FOUNDED 1830

SAMUELFRENCH-LONDON.CO.UK
SAMUELFRENCH.COM

Perfect Pitch

First presented at the Stephen Joseph Theatre, Scarborough 1998 season and subsequently toured by Hull Truck Theatre Company with the following cast:

Ron	James Hornsby
Yvonne	Kate Anthony
Grant	Adrian Hood
Steph	Samantha Hardcastle

Directed by **John Godber**
Designed by **Pip Leckenby**
Production Manager Graham Hawkins
Original music by James Pattison

The action takes place over a few days at a caravan park on the North Yorkshire coast of England and at a local theatre (inset scene)

The author has agreed that if amateur theatre companies think their audiences would feel uncomfortable with the strong language contained in *Perfect Pitch* then they are at liberty to tone it down.

It is not necessary to have a second caravan on stage and this can be suggested as being slightly off-stage.

Synopsis of Scenes

ACT I
Scene 1   A scorching summer's day
Scene 2   Minutes later
Scene 3   Twenty minutes later
Scene 4   Fifteen minutes later
Scene 5   Five minutes later
Scene 6   Five minutes later
Scene 7   An hour later
Scene 8   Evening
Scene 9   Half an hour later
Scene 10   The next morning
Scene 11   Later that day
Scene 12   Evening. Later
Scene 13   Early the next evening
Scene 14   Later that evening
Scene 15   Later that night

Act II
Scene 1   Early morning
Scene 2   Several hours later
Scene 3   Later that afternoon
Scene 4   Later
Scene 5   Later. Evening
Scene 6   An hour later
Scene 7   Half an hour later
Scene 8   Three hours later

Other plays by John Godber
published by Samuel French Ltd:

April in Paris
Blood Sweat and Tears
Departures
Gym and Tonic
Happy Families
It Started With a Kiss
Lucky Sods
Passion Killers
Salt of the Earth
Teechers
Unleashed
Up 'n' Under
Up 'n' Under II
Weekend Breaks

ACT I

A caravan site. A scorching summer's day

The east coast of North Yorkshire. A large green plot of grass. A caravan is positioned on stage. It has been cut away so that we can see inside. All the equipment for the caravan is new

Ron, a middle-aged, retired comprehensive school headmaster, is attempting to push this caravan on to its pitch. He wears sloppy clothes and a sun hat. Definitely not the outdoor type. Yvonne, his attractive wife, a few years younger, conducts the scene

Seagulls and crashing waves can be heard throughout

Yvonne Swing it!
Ron What?
Yvonne Swing it!
Ron I am!
Yvonne Pull it right round, it's not even straight. Come on, Ron, put your back into it.
Ron Is it moving?
Yvonne Swing it!
Ron Swing it? I'll swing you if you keep on.

Yvonne finds this amusing

Yvonne You're a mile off the pitch, you should have come back a bit, the man said come back a few yards, I kept saying.
Ron (*with a big effort*) Is that any better?
Yvonne Just swing it!
Ron (*with another big effort*) Argh!

Music. Black-out

SCENE 2

Minutes later

Ron has his arms under the front of the van and he is trying to force it sideways. It will not budge

Ron It must be there now, surely?
Yvonne No.
Ron I can hear my heart racing.
Yvonne It's not coming…
Ron This is what the car's for, you know?
Yvonne If you could back it and swing it, it would be perfect.
Ron If I could back it and swing it I'd be in the bloody Olympics.
Yvonne It's not even moving.
Ron Something is. I think I've pulled my stomach.
Yvonne Try and rock it.
Ron Rock it?
Yvonne You're nearly there.
Ron You're the fitness freak, you should be doing this. (*He gives in, exhausted*) Is that any better?
Yvonne I kept saying left.
Ron I kept turning left.
Yvonne No, you turned right when I said left. I said left but you turned right. I said left hand down.
Ron When I put my left hand down, Yvonne, I went right.
Yvonne Well, I did say left.
Ron (*breathless*) Never mind what you said, is that any good?

Music. Black-out

SCENE 3

Twenty minutes later

Ron stands looking at the caravan. Yvonne looks across the pitch. She is concerned

Yvonne I don't know if I wouldn't prefer it over there.
Ron You can park the damn thing next time.
Yvonne I thought it was going to go over the cliff!
Ron It nearly did.

Yvonne Why are you so useless at practical things?
Ron I felt such a pillock, was everybody watching?
Yvonne Not everyone. Just the site warden!
Ron I bet he can spot first-timers a mile off.
Yvonne I said you'd dropped it too short, but you wouldn't listen.

Ron surveys the location

Ron So this is it? Cliff Top Caravan site? Well, one thing's for sure, it's on a cliff top!
Yvonne Shall we get the gas on?
Ron It looks like a quiet site anyway.
Yvonne All the recommended ones were fully booked. I just looked in the *Yellow Pages* and phoned up.
Ron At least we're away from everyone else.
Yvonne Thank God! They'll not be able to see you making a fool of yourself.
Ron Exactly! (*He holds his stomach*) Do you know, I think I've ruptured myself towing that about, to be honest. I've ripped all across my stomach.
Yvonne Do you think we'll be all right here?
Ron Well, I'm not towing it about anymore.
Yvonne No, I mean on this site?
Ron Why shouldn't we?
Yvonne Well, it's not exactly La Rochelle, is it?
Ron I thought we'd agreed on this.
Yvonne You agreed.
Ron You agreed as well.
Yvonne A trial run. I said.
Ron This is a trial run.
Yvonne I thought we'd go in the back field, and then have our first real go in France.
Ron What sense would there have been putting it on the back field, that's where we park it.
Yvonne Well, it would have been just enough.
Ron No, we're better off coming up here.
Yvonne I think it's so down-market, though.
Ron It's all right, it's perfect. Nobody to bother us.

A beat

Yvonne I mean, Claire and Barry bought a gîte with his redundancy money and look what we got?
Ron Well, you can't tour a gîte! You can try, but it's a hard tow.
Yvonne And he wasn't even the Head of School, was he?

Ron Why are you worried about what Claire and Barry do?

Yvonne Well, they always thought they were better than us.

Ron So what?

Yvonne Well, they will do now! I don't even know why you had to tell anyone we'd bought one.

Ron Well, it's a bit difficult to hide, isn't it? Especially when it's stuck to the back of your bloody car!

Yvonne They only came round to gloat.

Ron looks at the pitch

Ron I'll get the awning, shall I? Where is it?

Yvonne It's still in the car.

Ron Oh, hell... I thought we'd unpacked it. (*He turns to depart*)

Yvonne I told you not to park all the way down there.

Ron I didn't have much choice, did I? The warden told me not to park on the edge. You know what this coast's like, too much weight and we're in the sea. I'll probably cripple myself carrying it all the way up here, but... (*He sets off to exit*)

Yvonne Go get 'em, tiger!

Ron It's supposed to be a relaxing weekend. I've ruptured myself and lost three stone, and we've only been here twenty minutes.

Ron exits

Music. Black-out

SCENE 4

Fifteen minutes later

Yvonne is caught in motion as she sorts out tables and chairs

Ron enters, carrying a large awning sack, a few metal pegs and a hammer. He begins to sort out the awning and is speaking as he works

Ron Don't bother putting anything in the car on the way back, I'll carry everything, might as well.

Yvonne We've been lucky to get a pitch this far out when you think about it. I suppose I'm quite looking forward to it really.

Ron I'm not looking forward to putting this up. Where are the instructions?

Yvonne I've not seen them.

Ron Well, I haven't.
Yvonne Well, do you need 'em?
Ron Well, I might.
Yvonne Well, where are they?
Ron Well, I don't know. I put them somewhere safe.
Yvonne Where?
Ron If I knew where…
Yvonne Can't you try and put it up without?
Ron Well, I can try.
Yvonne Well, try that then.
Ron Yeah, because it looks so easy, doesn't it? It looks like a piece of cake.
Yvonne It can't be that bad, everyone else has got theirs up.

Ron takes the awning and its metal bits from the bag

Ron No bloody instructions! It'll probably be time for home before I get it up.
Yvonne Do you want a hand?
Ron No, you just stand there taking in the view, I'll see to it. I'll see to it if it kills me. Look at this lot!
Yvonne You'll enjoy it when everything's ready…
Ron When everything's ready it'll be dark.
Yvonne (*still looking at the coastline*) This is a great coastline. You can follow the length of the coast all along here, look. That's one good thing, I'll be able to get some runs in.
Ron You should try doing this if you want to keep fit. This is how they should train for the London Marathon, caravan pulling, and awning erecting, it's all cardiovascular work, Sally Gunnell recommends it apparently.
Yvonne You know I'd forgotten how beautiful it is up here. I haven't been to Scarborough since I was about seven. Mind you, all we did then was play bingo and eat fish and chips. I suppose it's good for the soul, back to nature and all that.
Ron Oh, you!
Yvonne What?

Ron is holding a number of pieces of string and metal

Ron It's hardly back to nature, is it? We've got a full electricity supply, gas central heating, and a toilet. We haven't even got that at home, I mean the car boot's full of food from Marks and plastic stuff from Betaware. We've not exactly come to camp out in a hole and eat rabbits, have we?
Yvonne Well, I haven't!
Ron Mind you, I don't think I'm going to be able to take advantage of the toilet anyway.

Yvonne Why not?

Ron I can't fit my legs in.

Yvonne They say it's only for use in emergencies anyway.

Ron It will be an emergency if I get in there, you'd have to call the fire brigade to get me out. Now is that the back or the front?

Music. Black-out

SCENE 5

Five minutes later

Ron is still struggling with the awning, it is all out over the pitch. Yvonne is looking at the sea view

Yvonne It looks like a nice run along that cliff edge.

Ron That's good, then.

Yvonne You should try it, you need some exercise.

Ron No, I'm fine, honestly. (*He is now completely under the awning, holding two metal sticks*)

Yvonne walks to pick up some plastic boxes of food and cutlery and takes them into the caravan and begins to unpack. Ron plays the entire scene from under the awning

Yvonne I think I'm beginning to unwind already. Are you?

Ron Completely.

Yvonne It's not too bad for space, you know. Cosy, I think.

Ron How the bloody hell…? (*He still struggles*) You couldn't just give us a hand?

Yvonne Sorry, love. I'm unpacking.

Music. Black-out

SCENE 6

Five minutes later

Lights come up and Ron is still under the awning. He is having no luck at all. Yvonne stands watching

Ron It just doesn't make sense.

Yvonne The man I bought it off was sixty-nine and had been caravanning all his life.

Ron And not once had he managed to get the awning up. Not in sixty-nine years. (*Easily*) This bastard, bastard thing.

Yvonne What's the problem?

Ron The instructions, we're lost without them, that's the problem.

Yvonne Well, don't lose your temper, they can hear you all over the site. We don't want to get thrown off, do we?

Ron We'll probably get thrown off for not putting the awning up, I think it's some kind of initiation ceremony.

Yvonne Do you want to leave it?

Ron Well, if we could possibly live without it I'd be grateful. There is no way this is going up without the instructions.

Yvonne Well, I've said leave it. I don't know why you have to keep going on about it. Throw it out of the way and just leave it. Don't let's have a scene.

Ron picks up the awning and deposits it under the caravan

Ron Well, I've passed the caravan parking, and failed the awning erecting miserably.

Yvonne You only just scraped a pass at caravan parking, though, didn't you?

Ron Yes, the story of my life.

Music. Black-out

SCENE 7

An hour later

Yvonne lays out a few bits of picnic-type food. Ron is looking around the pitch, taking in the whole stage. Yvonne has a bottle of wine

Ron Where did you say you were you going to run to, then?

Yvonne Right down the coast.

Ron To Folkestone?

Yvonne Do you want wine?

Ron I'll just have a can of beer. You have one if you want!

Yvonne takes the wine into the caravan. Ron gets a can of beer and pours it deliberately into a small glass

Yvonne Not for me.

Ron I don't know, three months without a drink?

Yvonne That's good.

Ron That is good. I'm not complaining. It's the act of a saint as far as I'm concerned. If I get through one night, I've done rather well.

They sit and relax. Things aren't so bad after all. Yvonne gets a script from the caravan and begins to study it

Mmm.

Yvonne Mmmm.

Ron Yes, not bad at all.

Yvonne That's us sorted, then.

Ron How's that going?

Yvonne Fine.

Ron What is it, *Pinafore*?

Yvonne *Mikado*!

Ron Who's doing it this time, is it Peter?

Yvonne George Moonie.

Ron He's tone deaf.

Yvonne He's not.

Ron He was tone deaf when he taught in the science department twenty years ago, and I bet he hasn't got much better.

Yvonne You should've stayed with the amateur dramatics, it would have given you something to do.

Ron I've got something to do. I'm going to learn how to put an awning up. That should take me at least two years.

Yvonne You used to enjoy it, didn't you?

Ron Yes, but I got fed up of the same old arguments. Can you remember? Endless discussions about whether Peter should call himself director or producer? And when he eventually got the show on it was just an excuse for a sly snog at the after show party and a cup of champagne from a plastic cup.

Yvonne Oh, you make it sound awful.

Ron It is usually.

Yvonne We're not that bad.

Ron You're not, but look at the others. Look at Barbara Scott?

Yvonne She used to be a professional.

Ron A professional what?

Yvonne They reckon she sang with a band.

Ron I don't think she was there for the singing.

Yvonne Ron?

Ron Well!

Yvonne I mean, her husband had left her for another man, that must have been crippling.

Ron Who for?

Yvonne I mean, what does that say about her?

Ron When we did *Guys and Dolls* she used to trap me in the corner of the wings. She was all over me. Talk about getting stage fright? I got wings fright with Barbara Scott. That's probably why her husband left her, she scared him to death. Living with a Kiwi front row would be heaven compared to living with Barbara. I bet she weighed fifty stone.

Yvonne You were such a good Big Julie though.

A beat

Ron Not as good as she would've been.

Music. Black-out

SCENE 8

Evening

A large, old, caravan, with an erected awning, has appeared next to Ron's (see Production Note p. v). Ron looks at it in exasperation

Yvonne enters. She has been for a walk

Yvonne Can you believe the weather?

Ron Look at this!

Yvonne I've just walked as far as Filey. It's lovely, isn't it?

Ron It would be if he hadn't pitched that there.

Yvonne Oh, right!

Ron All this space and he has to park it there.

Yvonne Who is it?

Ron God only knows. I fell asleep and when I woke up again there they were, awning up and every damn thing.

Yvonne There was a bit of a climb coming back.

Ron All this space.

Yvonne begins to take off her trainers

Yvonne Yes, that's going to be a nice run in the mornings. Right on the cliff top.

Ron Awning up and everything.

Yvonne What did you say?

Ron Must have got that awning up in no time. Mind you, it's not like that one of ours, is it?

Yvonne Did you see them?

Ron I haven't seen a soul.

Yvonne Well, they're not affecting us, are they?

Ron All the space on this edge and somebody has to park there.

Yvonne Maybe they wanted the view as well.

Ron I don't like them being that near!

Yvonne That's what happens on caravan sites, other people pull up at the side of you and you start to have conversations, that's why people go away, they don't want to stay in their back garden completely hidden from the world, it's called society, Ron. That's why I wanted to go to France, at least there was a chance of meeting somebody different.

Ron Different to what?

Yvonne To the bloody English!

Ron Oh, we're off.

Yvonne Well…! (*She sits*)

Ron has another can of beer

Ron Oh, well, there's not a lot we can do, is there? Can I tempt you?

Yvonne Three months and two days since my last one.

Ron Twenty minutes, and three seconds since mine.

Yvonne Put a tape on?

Ron Absolutely!

Yvonne finds a tape and the cassette player from a cupboard or drawer in the caravan

Yvonne A little bit of ambience.

Ron What have you got?

Yvonne Classic Experience.

Ron Which?

Yvonne *Nocturne*!

Ron What else!

Yvonne A little adagio and we'll be well away…

Ron It's beautiful here, I'll tell you that.

Yvonne I love this.

They slip on a Classic Experience cassette. They sit as Debussy's Clair de Lune *plays*

Ron Oh, yes.

Yvonne I take it all back.

Ron Not bad so far, the old caravanning.
Yvonne No, I'll give you that. I love this piece.
Ron Oh, dear!
Yvonne Lovely!
Ron Mmm.
Yvonne Very nice.
Ron Very.
Yvonne Very very nice.

They begin to hum and conduct the music. As they do this we hear the sound of love-making coming from inside the other caravan. It is very vocal and excitable. It is the voice of Steph, a coarse young northern woman

Steph Oh, oh… Oh, oh, oh, oh…
Ron This is a very good recording.
Yvonne It is actually.
Ron To say it's tape.
Yvonne Very good to say it's tape, isn't it?
Ron I think it's one of those digitally re-mastered jobs.
Yvonne I don't mind tape really…
Steph Oh, oh, oh, oh, oh…

Ron tries to listen to the music, but he can hear Steph's moans too

Ron What's that?
Yvonne What?
Ron That…
Yvonne What?
Ron Turn it down a bit.

They turn down the cassette player. And we can now hear the love-making very clearly

Steph Oh! Oh! Oh!
Ron That!
Yvonne Oh, well.
Ron Oh, right!
Yvonne Mmmm!

Ron gets up to go and look off stage

Yvonne Where are you going?
Ron For a look.

Yvonne Ron!
Ron Look at that.
Yvonne What?
Ron Amazing, the whole bloody caravan's rocking.
Yvonne Come away.
Steph Oh, oh, oh, oh, oh…

Ron is transfixed, looking at the other caravan

Ron Nobody makes that sort of noise, do they?
Yvonne We did.
Ron You're joking, aren't you?
Yvonne We did.
Ron Yvonne, we used to do it at my mother's and didn't even make a sound, you know how light a sleeper my mum is. I was holding my breath some of the time. It's a wonder I didn't die.
Steph Oooooooooh!
Ron That is just…
Yvonne Wonderful, by the sound of it.
Ron The whole sodding van is moving. If they're not careful it'll be over the edge. (*He comes back to Yvonne*) And what are you grinning at?
Yvonne What?
Ron You, you're grinning.
Yvonne I am not.
Ron You've got a right grin on your bloody face.
Yvonne I haven't.
Ron You're positively glowing.
Yvonne That's the fresh air.
Steph Oh, oh, oh…
Ron That's pollution, that is!
Steph Don't stop, don't stop, yes, oh!
Yvonne You're the one who's grinning.
Ron I'm not.
Yvonne You are.
Steph Oh, oh, oh, oh!!
Ron This is insane. (*He shouts*) Pack it in! Turn the radio up.
Yvonne Don't you think it reminds you of the good old days.
Ron What, the television programme?
Yvonne Don't be daft.

A beat

Ron We've never made a noise like that, never ever.

Yvonne Oh, we have.

Ron We haven't.

Yvonne What about when we went to stay at Jeff and Margi's?

Ron I'd only just met you!

Yvonne Well, maybe he's just met her?

Ron I had to make a lot of noise to cover the sound of my chest wheezing. I got asthma!

Yvonne Another romantic night.

Ron Maybe it's two women.

Yvonne Maybe it's two men? Maybe it's Barbara Scott's husband? Sounds like they're having a good time whoever it is!

Ron Turn the radio up a bit, it's making me feel sick.

Yvonne Oh, sometimes!

Steph Oh, oh, oh, oh!

Ron No, honestly. That is sickening.

Yvonne It isn't.

Ron I mean, what are they doing?

Yvonne Just put your mind off it.

Ron Easier said than done.

Yvonne It's only natural.

Ron It doesn't sound it!

Steph Oh, oh, yes, oh, yes!

A beat

Ron I have never made a woman moan like that.

Yvonne (*referring to the* Mikado *book*) I'm trying to learn this.

Ron Except at college. I was noisy at college.

Yvonne Oh, here we go.

Steph Oh, oh, oh, yes...

Ron The trouble was, it was me who made all the noise. I was with this girl once...

Yvonne Spare me the details.

Steph Oh, oh, oh, yes, oh...

Ron I was moaning like hell, because I'd got my feet caught in the end of the bed!

Steph Yes, yes, yes.

Ron I always made all the noise, come to think of it.

Steph Yes. Yes. Arghhh!

Silence

Ron Well, that's that, then.

Yvonne You can relax now?

A beat

Ron They must be knackered.

Yvonne Beats jogging, so they say.

Ron They must be absolutely bloody shattered… (*He gets up and saunters over to the caravan*)

Yvonne Come away.

Ron You can't keep that up for that length of time without it taking its toll on your health surely.

Yvonne Well, it's obviously new to them, whoever it is.

Ron saunters back to base

Ron You never ever made much of a noise, did you?

Yvonne Meaning?

Ron I was just thinking.

Yvonne Leave it.

Ron Thank God they've finished anyway.

Yvonne You never know, we might be doing the same!

Ron Oh, yes?

Yvonne Never know your luck.

Ron I don't think so. I can't fit in the bed for a start.

Yvonne How do you know?

Ron Because I tried when you went for a walk. I put the whole bed down. If I sleep straight out I'll end up with a flat head and if I slept on my side I'll be like Quasimodo in the morning.

Silence

Steph Oh, oh, oh, oh, oh, oh…

Ron Not again! Please not again!

Steph Oh, oh, oh, yes, oh.

Ron Oh, come on, this is ridiculous!

Music. Black-out

SCENE 9

Half an hour later

Silence, Ron is in the caravan. Yvonne is outside. Both are packing away their bits and bobs

Steph appears from her caravan. She is a rough-looking girl in her mid twenties who smokes. She speaks in a coarse northern brogue

Ron I don't know how they even managed it, to be honest.
Yvonne What?
Ron You can't swing a cat in here!
Yvonne You can put the beds down in a minute.
Ron I think that there might be a bottleneck for the sink, every time I turn around, I bang my knees or something.
Steph Bloody hell, warm tonight, in't it?
Yvonne Sorry?
Steph I say, a nice night!
Yvonne Lovely.
Steph Yeah.
Yvonne Warm!
Steph Bloody boiling, in't it?
Yvonne It is, isn't it?

A beat

   Nice site.
Steph You been before?
Yvonne No, this is our first time.
Steph New van!
Yvonne Yes.
Steph Look at ours. Dropping to bits. Looks good, yours.
Yvonne Oh, thanks.
Steph Three hundred quid off Grant's brother, ours.
Yvonne Well, Ron's just taken early retirement from teaching so we——
Steph No, it's not bad up here.
Yvonne So we thought——
Steph This site's a bit dull, but at least it's cheap.
Yvonne Give it a go, you know, thought about it and——
Steph We come up a lot. I like to do the clubs. Grant dun't like leaving the dogs but...
Yvonne Ever so nice, the coast.

Ron comes out of the caravan

    Oh, this is Ron. This is…?
Steph Steph.
Ron Oh, right?
Steph Are you all right, then?
Ron Yes.
Steph That's all right, then.
Ron Yes, I'm fine.

Silence

Yvonne Just saying, Steph comes up here a lot.
Ron Really?
Yvonne She says the site's a bit dull, though.
Ron (*deadpan*) Oh, I wouldn't say that, it's been very interesting so far.
Steph You have to make your own entertainment.
Ron So I gather.
Steph There's a club on the site next door, if you're into karaoke and that.
Ron One for you, Yvonne.
Yvonne You never know.
Steph Eh?
Ron Yvonne sings.
Steph Oh, right then!
Yvonne Well, you know…
Ron Gilbert and Sullivan.
Steph Oh, hell…
Ron She's good actually…

A beat

Steph Anyway. Just go for a shower. It gets a bit sweaty inside in this
    weather.
Ron That's right.
Steph There's quite a lot going off in town, you know, if you…
Ron That's right…
Steph Anyway, see you later…

    Steph strides off towards the shower block

Ron Mmm.
Yvonne Well.
Ron Difficult to know what to say.

Yvonne I could see that.

Ron Well, what are you supposed to say? How was it for you? I can't wait to see what the other half is like.

Yvonne Oh, please!

Ron You mean you're not interested?

As they sit, Grant ambles on to the stage. He is a man the same age as Ron, but distinctly rounded, aggressive and dirty. He wears a vest, some dirty tracksuit bottoms, and is sweating. He is frightening

Grant Huh!

Yvonne Evening.

Grant Huh.

Grant exits

Yvonne So there!

Ron He's your man.

Yvonne Talkative.

Ron He's obviously breathless, the poor sod. I'm going to see what he has for his breakfast. Whatever he has, I'll have two of.

Yvonne He must be at least your age.

Ron I wondered what those tyres were hanging from trees for when we came in. Now I know.

Yvonne Really?

Ron They're obviously for him to swing on.

Music. Black-out

SCENE 10

The next morning

Yvonne is tidying up the remains of last night's snack

Steph enters. She puts up a couple of chairs, outside her awning

Steph I tell you sommat, I feel like shit this morning.

Yvonne Really?

Steph Didn't get back till gone two!

Yvonne I was up at six. Just me on the sands. Well, me and a dog, jogging... You OK?

Steph I've got such a head!
Yvonne Oh, dear.
Steph I was mixing it. We went down to the Nelson.
Yvonne I've got some tablets, if you...
Steph (*lighting a cigarette*) No, one of these and I'll be sorted.

A beat

You say you've been running?
Yvonne Just sorting out a course.
Steph What for?
Yvonne I want to do next year's marathon.
Steph Oh, hell!
Yvonne That's what I'm beginning to think.
Steph Run for a bus and I'm knackered. I keep saying I'm gunna give up these, but...
Yvonne Oh, you'd get into it if you put your mind to it.

A beat

Steph You sleep all right, then?
Yvonne Not bad, thanks, but it's not really my thing, I'm afraid. I'm making the best of a bad job really.
Steph Why's that? It's a lovely van, I wish we'd got one like it.
Yvonne Well, it's OK, but...
Steph Swap you!
Yvonne I don't think Ron'd be keen, it's become his pride and joy.
Steph What's up, then?
Yvonne Well, nothing. Not a lot to do, though!
Steph There's some good shops in Scarborough. There's a Pizza Hut and all if you fancy...
Yvonne Well, it's not that so much...
Steph What then?
Yvonne We were going to France but Ron changed his mind at the last minute.
Steph Oh, right. I've only ever been to Calais.
Yvonne Oh, it's nice, isn't it?
Steph Didn't see much of it, we just went to a supermarket and then we came straight back. Nine hours, there and back!
Yvonne Really!
Steph Yeah. Grant doesn't like being away from the dogs.
Yvonne Have you got kennels?
Steph Just in the garden, he breeds bull-terriers.

Yvonne Oh, right.

Steph He's dog mad. He's on about seeing some of his dog mates on Saturday, so I says I'm going down town then.

Yvonne Good for you!

Steph Well, I'm not going to sit and listen to them bore each other senseless. And I don't fancy staying here by myself so...

Yvonne You're having a night on the town, then?

Steph Hey, don't knock it!

Yvonne I wasn't.

Steph Yeah. I thought I'd sample the nightlife.

Yvonne Good for you!

Steph Dead right!

A beat

Yvonne Well, I don't know what we're doing this weekend yet!

Steph You can come out with me if you want?

Yvonne What?

Steph You can come down town with me!

Yvonne Oh, right.

Steph Do you want?

Yvonne Well...

Steph I'm only going to have a pizza or sommat.

Yvonne Oh, really?

Steph If you fancy a change.

Yvonne Well, I think Ron might not...

Steph I mean, might even see if there's a show on or sommat, I usually go and see sommat.

Yvonne Take advantage!

Steph Have you seen the Grumbleweeds, they might be on?

Yvonne I have actually...

Steph There must be sommat on at the Futurist?

Yvonne I suppose so.

Steph I'll have a look, shall I?

Yvonne Well, yes, I suppose there must be something on, it's high season, isn't it?

Steph I'm going into Scarborough, I can get some tickets, if you want?

Yvonne Well, I...

Steph Please yourself!

Yvonne Well...?

Steph I mean. I'm not forcing you. It's just that he dun't like me going down town on my own.

Yvonne No, right.

Steph Anyway!

Yvonne No, no, that's fine, I'll come for a pizza.

Steph Yeah?

Yvonne Ron'll just have to sit and read. Hang on.

Steph What?

Yvonne Actually, I think I've got a leaflet for the Futurist. Shall I have a look? (*She goes towards the caravan*)

Steph (*shouting*) I'm not into Gilbert O Sullivan or opera or owt, so!

Yvonne Hang on. I picked one up with a load of other stuff. Hang on. I got some when we first arrived. I always do, I always get a handful of leaflets. I just grab them from the tourist place, do you? (*She goes into the caravan and pulls out a leaflet for the Futurist Theatre*) Here we are. Let's have a look. Roy Chubby Brown.

Steph Oh, I've seen him, he's brilliant!

Yvonne Is he really?

Steph Funny.

Yvonne Let's have a look! No, I don't think there's anything. Oh, Tommy Steele, oh, we've missed him! Oh, that's a shame, I would have fancied that. I like him! Let's have a look. Steve Coogan, gone! Ah, Saturday! One night only, "The Ultimate Female Fantasy". Ladies Only. No, I don't think it's for us, do you?

Steph What is it?

Yvonne A strip act, that's not what we're after, is it?

Steph Why not?

Yvonne Well…

Steph Should be a laugh. I've always wanted to see one.

Yvonne Well, I don't think it's for me!

Steph Why not?

Yvonne No, not for me…

A beat

Steph Can I have a look at that. (*She looks at the leaflet*) Oh, yeah. A Female Fantasy show! Hey, they look good on the poster anyway.

Yvonne Yes, but is it art?

Steph No, but I bet it's a laugh.

Yvonne Do you think so?

Steph Don't you fancy it?

Yvonne Are you joking?

Steph I bet it's great.

Yvonne What about, erm…?

Steph Oh, he'll not be bothered…

Yvonne Oh!

Steph What's up, won't he like you going?

Yvonne It's not that...
Steph I mean, it's only a bit of fun, isn't it?
Yvonne I don't think it's me, though.
Steph If you don't want to come...

A beat

Yvonne I'd better forget about it, actually.
Steph Well, please yourself, but they've got nothing that you haven't seen before, have they?
Yvonne Who knows?
Steph Well, think about it.
Yvonne I don't...
Steph We'll just have sommat to eat, then. I mean, I can't go on my own anyway, can I? Not to sommat like that, I mean what do you think I am, a pervert?

Steph exits as Ron comes from the washroom with the newspaper

Ron Bloody hay fever. I thought the sea air might sort it out, but it obviously hasn't. What's it like down there?
Yvonne Wonderful on the sands. I'm going to do a three mile jog in the morning and a ten mile run in the afternoon.
Ron I tried to phone the firm by the way. The man said, get some two by one and fix it yourself. I nearly went ballistic. All that money and he said fix it yourself! What are you doing, planning an outing?
Yvonne Just seeing what was on in Scarborough. She's invited me out for a pizza.
Ron Well, that's nice of her! They're not too bad, are they?
Yvonne Is the washroom busy?
Ron No, no, it's quiet, and it's clean, if you get there in the morning it's spotless. Fix it yourself, he said. A brand new caravan and the bloody bed breaks. I wouldn't mind, we weren't doing anything!
Yvonne I'll pop and get myself sorted, then.

Yvonne jogs off

Ron sits and looks at a paper he has with him

Grant comes from his caravan

Ron Morning.
Grant Huh.
Ron Ah, well.

Grant Eh?
Ron What?
Grant Eh?
Ron Nothing.
Grant Oh.
Ron Only morning.
Grant Oh.
Ron That's all.
Grant Thee brake's not on.
Ron I beg your pardon!

Grant goes near to Ron's van and inspects it

Grant Thee brake's not on. It's a wonder thy an't run backwards during the
   night.
Ron Oh shit, that's the brake, is it?
Grant And tha' wants to put that waste tank on its side, it'll be better like that.
Ron Oh, right. It didn't say on the instructions.
Grant And get some bits of wood and put them under your supports,
   otherwise you'll ruin the pitch for somebody else.
Ron Oh right, yes!
Grant Then you can get more purchase.
Ron Thanks for that.
Grant Tha's not been in't van before, then?
Ron No, no!
Grant No, I thought not!

Birds twitter

   Grant exits

Ron watches Grant go then goes to change the waste tank

Music. Black-out

SCENE 11

Later that day

*Yvonne is coming back from her shower and fixes up a small washing line.
She hangs her smalls on a it. She is wearing hot pants, looks flushed and
radiant. She has recently finished a long run*

Grant comes to her. And watches her

Yvonne sings to herself

Yvonne Hiya. Gave me a shock. You OK. Nice day. Ron's just gone for the phone, he can't get a signal here, he likes to phone the girls, see how things are at home. Is there anything wrong?

Grant I was just seeing if he'd seen to that waste tank.

Yvonne Oh, right.

Grant He'd got it the wrong way up.

Yvonne Yes, he's not the best in the world at outdoor things. He thinks he is, but...

Grant He'll learn.

Yvonne Lovely today again, isn't it?

A beat

Grant So she says you're going to see some strippers or sommat?

Yvonne Well, actually...

Grant Ah, you buggers!

Yvonne I'm not sure yet.

Grant That's what she said.

Yvonne Maybe.

Grant Well, you'd better tell her.

Yvonne Oh, right.

Grant You seen 'em before?

Yvonne No.

Grant I bet she wets hersen, she gets that excited over owt like that.

Yvonne Really?

Grant Load of bollocks to me, but...

Ron enters on the end of this line

Ron Couldn't get through, I had to walk right to the site office and ring from a land line. Just been to phone the girls. We've got three. Daughters. Girls, well, little women now!

Grant I was just checking your waste tank, see if you'd done it.

Ron Not yet.

Grant Get it done, man, do the job right!

Ron Yes, I had to walk all the way down there to make a bloody phone call. Got this mobile, useless half the time, aren't——

Grant I was just saying, you'd better be on your guard when they've been down to watch them strippers. They might come back with some right ideas.

Grant exits

Ron What's all that about?

Yvonne She asked me if I wanted to go for a pizza. I said yes, and now she's gone and got some tickets for a male strip show.

Ron Oh, nice.

Yvonne I told her not to bother.

Ron Why don't you go another night, to see something decent?

Yvonne It's Roy Chubby Brown! We've just missed Tommy Steele.

Ron Well, tell her you don't want to go...

Yvonne I did! But Grant's going out with some mates and she'll be going around town on her own.

Ron Oh, right!

Yvonne Well, it doesn't seem right, does it?

Ron I thought you hated all that stuff.

Yvonne Well, I don't know, do I, I've never been, have I?

Ron So, I'll be sat reading David Lodge and you're going to be watching an officer and a gentlemen get his kit off!

Yvonne Sounds like you know all about it?

Ron Some of the science department went to something like it!

Yvonne And?

Ron Well, they said it was a disappointment actually! Except for Pauline West, she loved it. She went back the next night I think. But you know Pauline, she can't get enough of it! Well, I'd better see to this bloody waste tank before he beats me up. (*He puts the waste tank on its side, then calls across to Grant*) I've done it!

Black-out

Scene 12

Evening. Later

Ron, Yvonne, Steph and Grant are sitting around the small plastic table. Steph smokes heavily. Grant has a can of beer. Things are unnecessarily friendly between them. We should get the impression that this conversation has been going on some time

Yvonne You'll not believe this, so anyway, when we eventually got to bed, Ron turned over and the bed split in half.

Ron It did. Snap!

Yvonne I thought his back had gone.

Ron I thought it was my stomach.

Yvonne He phoned them up, didn't you?

Ron I phoned them up, this morning.

Yvonne The man at the firm said, just get a bit of wood…

Ron Fourteen thousand quid. Cash.

Steph Cash?

Yvonne The man said just get a piece of two by one…

Ron Two by one, he said.

Yvonne And mend it yourself.

Steph Mend it yourself?

Yvonne I thought, Ron mend anything, he's no good at anything practical, intellectual yes, but practical things, no way.

Steph What were you doing to break the bed?

Ron Just rolling over?

Steph Argh?

Yvonne He's no good at all with his hands.

Steph Not very good with your hands, then?

Ron I can put a shelf up.

Yvonne If pushed.

Steph Grant does all our stuff, don't you?

No reply

He does all our stuff.

Yvonne No, not with Ron, if we're having any decorating done we have to get somebody in. And I don't understand why … because his father was a painter on the council, wasn't he?

Grant Have you seen the gob on her?

Silence

Yvonne I'm sorry?

Grant Your gob, it's non stop, in't it?

Yvonne What about it?

Grant She's got a right gob on her an't she, like a bloody opera singer or sommat! I mean, she's got like a singer's mouth, an't she?

Ron She's got perfect pitch, haven't you?

Grant Oh ay. What do you sing, then?

Yvonne All sorts.

Ron She read music at Oxford.

Yvonne She?

Ron Sorry.

Grant Sing sommat then.

Yvonne Not here.

Grant I bet she's shit, aren't you?

Ron We went on a cruise last year, and she won a talent contest, didn't you?

Yvonne I'm not singing here, Ron.

Steph I wouldn't mind going on a cruise.

Grant Well, you've had that.

All laugh

Ron And us, we're not going on another one.

Yvonne It cost us a fortune…

Grant You pay that in cash?

Ron It's not bad, you know, a cruise, they've got all the stuff.

Grant It's the people, though, in't it?

Ron Well?

Steph They're all a bit…

Ron Well, we weren't.

Grant Yeah, she's got a good mouth, an't she? I thought when I saw her, I thought. She's got a singer's mouth that woman.

Steph He won't stop in a hotel.

Yvonne No?

Steph He hates hotels, don't you?

Grant suddenly rises

Grant Right, come on, then!

Steph Are we going?

Grant Go and have a walk, and have some fish and chips. Do you want owt fetching?

Ron No, I…

Yvonne We're fine, thanks.

Grant Right, come on.

Grant moves off. Steph lingers

Steph Don't forget to get your ticket off me…

Grant Ay, she dun't want you changing your mind and her havin' to go herself! Come on!

Steph I'm comin'.

Steph walks over to Grant and they walk off

Ron and Yvonne sit in silence. Ron sips his can of beer

Ron Mmmm.

Yvonne What?

Ron Interesting.

Yvonne The man's a pig.

Ron He's all right.

Yvonne Try and get to know 'em?

Ron It takes all sorts.

Yvonne Oh, he's just thick, Ron, admit it.

Ron He's all right.

Yvonne If he went to watch the Sea Lion show he probably wouldn't understand it! That's real life, that is. We're actually living on another planet, aren't we?

Ron They're not in the fast lane, are they?

Yvonne I don't think that they're in any lane, to be brutally honest.

A beat

Ron She's all right though.

Yvonne Meaning?

Ron What?

Yvonne Meaning?

Ron Meaning, she's all right. She's great, full of it.

Yvonne Oh, leave it.

Ron What?

Yvonne That you feel sorry for her.

Ron I never said a word.

Yvonne You don't have to.

Ron I have never said a word!

Yvonne You can't save every disadvantaged kid in the world, Ron, that's what nearly killed you at school!

Ron Some people just don't seem to stand a chance, do they?

Yvonne Don't be so patronizing.

Ron I wasn't being, was I, I was being observant.

Yvonne Well, thankfully I'm not from your sort of background, so I don't have a problem with it. People either make something of their lives or they don't, and that's how it works. Don't make it your burden.

Ron I'm not.

Yvonne Good.

Ron And anyway, don't tell me what to do.

Yvonne What?

Ron Don't tell me what to do.

Yvonne I wasn't.

Ron Yes, you were.

Yvonne Well, I'm sorry.

Ron OK, fine.

Yvonne Go on, then. Take on the burden of the dysfunctional if that's what rings your bell.

Ron They're not dysfunctional. Now you're being patronizing.

Yvonne Well, is there any wonder?

Ron Well, you don't like it when I tell you what to do, do you? I mean, if I said: "don't go and see those strippers", you wouldn't like it, would you?

Yvonne Oh, so that's what this is about?

Ron No!

Yvonne I just wish you wouldn't be so...

Ron What?

Yvonne Anal!

Ron Anal?

Yvonne But you are!

Ron Go on your run if you're going. I'll do all this. Even though it has an element of practicality about it. I'm sure I'll be able to do it. It'll be a challenge.

Yvonne I can't believe you're being like this!

Ron Like what?

Yvonne You're repressed. That's your problem, always have been.

Ron Where did all that come from, touched a sensitive nerve, have I?

Yvonne If you're going to make such a song and dance about it, I won't go. I won't even go for a pizza, I'll stay here and change the chemical toilet or something!

Ron Do you want to go?

Yvonne No.

Ron Oh, come on!

Yvonne You've never seen a stripper, have you?

Ron Years ago. Sadly!

Yvonne Funny!

Ron Look, what can I say? I can't win. If I say I don't want you to go, I look repressive, if I say I want you to go I look like I'm not bothered.

Yvonne What are you scared of? Comparisons?

Ron Spare me that. My hopes of being Mister Body Beautiful for the East Coast evaporated when I was twenty-one! I've seen myself in the mirror, and it's not pretty, you should know that.

Yvonne Look, hundreds of women go, thousands.

Ron I know and I'm not stopping you from going. But you don't seem to be hearing me!

Yvonne I'm only going to see how the women behave.

Ron So you are going now?

Yvonne I'll not go.

Ron But you want to go, don't you?

Silence

Tell me the truth.
Yvonne Yes.
Ron Why?
Yvonne Look, why are we arguing about this rubbish?
Ron We're not arguing.
Yvonne It's a bit of fun, that's all.
Ron A bit of fun, oh right, is that all it is?
Yvonne Oh, Ron, it is.
Ron Of course it is, how could it be anything else?
Yvonne Come on...?
Ron When I started teaching I was on cover for a difficult fifth year group—as it was then known. I'd got them working and I was sat at the front writing up some notes for my M. Ed., as it happens. And these two lads got talking. One of them had been to a do at a golf club somewhere, Bradford I think. They'd had a comic on and then a stripper, and then another stripper. Then a bloke came around with the hat apparently, asking if they'd like to see an act, you know...
Yvonne I've got the picture.
Ron Well, you can imagine what happened.
Yvonne Yes, I can, thank you!
Ron Anyway, according to this lad everybody ended up on stage, including him, fifteen he must have been. I don't know what really went on, but by God the image has been imprinted on my brain for years. It was a brilliant laugh, he said. A brilliant laugh. And do you know what, it just started as a bit of fun.
Yvonne So what are you saying?
Ron I'm saying it's a cruel world.
Yvonne Oh, the oracle speaks!
Ron Come out of your bubble.
Yvonne I don't live in a bubble.
Ron Book clubs, coffee mornings, amateur dramatics and découpage? Early music? Yvonne, bloody hell, you live the life of Riley. And now you want to go down into the swamp!
Yvonne The swamp? Oh, come on!
Ron Well?
Yvonne And you don't live the life of Riley, do you? We've just bought that sodding thing for fourteen grand cash!
Ron I see more of real life than you. Well, I did.
Yvonne Yes, and look what it did to you?

Ron You go if you want. I can't stop you going, can I?

Yvonne stands to exit

Where are you going now?
Yvonne For a run.
Ron At this time?
Yvonne Why not?
Ron So what shall I do with this spare food, put it in the fridge or bin it?

Yvonne jogs off

Ron continues to put the rubbish into his plastic bag

Music. Black-out

SCENE 13

Early the next evening

Steph enters, she is very dolled up with far too much flesh showing. She looks distinctly cheap

Ron comes from his caravan

Steph She ready?
Ron Just gone to the shower block. She says there isn't enough light in here. You look nice.
Steph It's just a bit of slap.
Ron No, looks great.
Steph I've plastered it on, I want to get down there. Do you know, I'm shaking already. Mind you, once we've got a few drinks down us, we should be all right. Just think about us, down there watching all that flesh.
Ron I will do.
Steph Seems weird us down there and you up here reading a book or sommat!
Ron Well, I've done my galivanting.
Steph Oh ay?
Ron Oh ay, I've done my bit.
Steph What and you a headmaster?
Ron Never judge a book by its cover.
Steph Why's that, then?

Ron It's a saying.

Steph Oh, you're full of 'em, aren't you?

Ron What time does it start?

Steph The main act's on at eight.

Ron Oh right, I wonder if it'll have an interesting structure?

Yvonne enters, looking much more attractive than before and up for the night ahead

Yvonne You can't see a thing in there at this time of night, somebody's caked grass all over the mirror. Will this do. I mean I look like one of their mothers or something!

Steph She looks great, doesn't she?

Yvonne I don't.

Steph Just think when she gets back, Ron, she'll want to ravish you!

Ron What, more than she does now?

Steph Come on, let's go and see all them muscles. I bet you can't wait, can you?

Yvonne No, that's right.

Steph Don't wait up, hey, if we get near the front, we might never come back!

Ron If you get near the front, you might have an eye out.

Grant enters, he is dressed for the night too

Grant What've we got here, then?

Steph Arh, you're only jealous because you're not coming.

Grant Ah, well, I might come, that'd spoil it for you, wouldn't it?

Steph He would come and all him just to spite us!

Grant How do you know I'm not one of the strippers anyway?

Steph Well, if you are I want a chuffin' refund. What do you think?

Yvonne Oh, I don't know.

Grant I've got everything they've got, you needn't worry about that!

Steph Ay, but you've got some of it in the wrong place, love. You want to take some of that from round your middle and put it somewhere else.

Grant Go on, you cheeky get!

Steph I bet he's going to follow us, aren't you?

Grant You're joking, aren't you. Once those women down there catch sight of me, them stripper efforts would stand no chance.

Steph Oh, yeah?

Grant What do you reckon, Yvonne. Do I look all right?

Yvonne Better than he does. (*She is referring to Ron*)

Ron You two had better go if you're going. If you don't get there at the beginning, you won't be able to follow the plot, will you?

Yvonne I'll see you later, then!

The women begin to move off

I won't be late, ring the girls.
Ron You just go and have a good time. And don't look!
Steph That's the whole point, in't it?

Steph and Yvonne exit

A beat

Grant She's been wanting to go for ages.
Ron It's just a bit of fun, isn't it?
Grant She says they go the whole way. I saw a documentary about it!
They're just groups of lads who love the-sens, into t' body beautiful and
all that. Arse-wipes I think, I wouldn't piss on 'em if they were burning in
the street, half off 'em are queers anyway.
Ron You reckon?
Grant Half of 'em.
Ron Really?
Grant Queers.
Ron No worries there, then?

Grant farts loudly

Grant Get out and walk. Sea's calm, should be a nice night.
Ron You reckon?
Grant Tha can come down for a drink if tha wants?
Ron No, thanks. I'll just…
Grant Please thee-sen. (*He is offended by his own stink*) Good God, that
stinks! Sorry about that, better out than in!

Grant walks off

*Ron watches him go and then returns to his caravan and commences reading.
As he does, sexy pop music plays under and swells through to the following
scene*

SCENE 14

The Futurist Theatre

A corner of the stage is designated for the Futurist Theatre

Steph and Yvonne are watching the strip show. Both are drinking from bottles. Ron remains on stage for a while

Sexy pop music plays. As this happens the two women become completely engrossed in the show they are watching

Steph (*shouting*) Get it off! Come on, get it off. (*To Yvonne*), I like that one! The one with the tatoo!
Yvonne Oh no!
Steph What about the black one?
Yvonne No...
Steph Don't you like any of 'em?
Yvonne The one with long hair.
Steph Nice arse.
Yvonne Well, a big one anyway.
Steph Nice big arse. Just one night with that and what you wouldn't do! Get your bloody teeth into that and you'd be laughing.
Yvonne You might be, he wouldn't.
Steph Bite his bloody arse off!

Both women laugh uproariously

(*Shouting*) Come on, big arse, show us what you've got!
Yvonne Look at his stomach. Ron's was never like that.
Steph Get your pants off, big arse. Get 'em off and throw 'em over here! Oh, I like that one.
Yvonne Which one?
Steph The one with the chest.
Yvonne They've all got bloody chests...
Steph We'll have to get their autographs, won't we? Put some oil on it!

As the girls narrate the event, Ron decides to get ready for bed. He goes into the caravan and puts his pyjamas on

Come on, show us it, then!
Yvonne Come on!
Steph Get 'em off.

Yvonne (*to Steph*) Do they take it all off?
Steph They would if I had anything to do with it.
Yvonne Oh, he's nice, this one!
Steph Slow, slower. Oh, yes, that's it, that's it, nice and slow.

Throughout this, Ron is pulling on some styleless pyjamas, and he crawls into bed

Yvonne Nice.
Steph Firm. Oh God…
Yvonne Turn around, turn around.
Steph Full Monty, Full Monty…
Yvonne Yes … ah, ah… Ah my God! Brilliant!

They both applaud

Steph Do you want another drink?
Yvonne Well, I shouldn't really.
Steph Are you enjoying it?
Yvonne No. It's absolutely awful!
Steph Hey, wait until it gets really going, they haven't even started yet!

Pop music swells. The Lights fade to black

SCENE 15

Later that night

The caravan site is quiet. Ron is asleep

Grant stumbles back on to the site. He is quite drunk. He sings badly to himself. He has a couple of dead rabbits with him. He sits on the chairs outside Ron's caravan. He switches on the cassette player and J S Bach's Sheep May Safely Graze *plays*

Grant Not bad! (*He leaves a rabbit for Ron*)

Steph and Yvonne enter, drunk. A torch lights their way

Steph Sssh.
Yvonne Ron must be asleep.
Steph You'll have to go and waken him.

Yvonne Oh, heck.

Grant Back, then?

Steph Good night?

Grant Mate of mine gave me some rabbits, there's one for you.

Yvonne For me?

Grant Have you ever had a bit of rabbit?

Yvonne No.

Grant It's nice is rabbit.

Yvonne Oh, thanks...

Grant Skin it, and you'll be all right with that.

Yvonne Skin it?

Grant What was it like, then?

Steph Hey, this one here is off her head!

Yvonne It's not me, it's you.

Steph Got her up on stage.

Grant Yeah?

Yvonne I didn't know what was going on, to be honest.

Steph She was putting oil all over 'em!

Yvonne Oh, no, come on, he made me.

Steph I think she could have been well in there.

Yvonne I think I could.

Steph They just grabbed her, didn't they?

Grant Must have thought she needed it.

Yvonne Bloody embarrassing, wasn't it?

Steph No.

Yvonne No?

Steph Yes!

Yvonne Yes!

Steph You should've seen her face. I mean, there's five hundred women there and they pick her.

Yvonne I couldn't believe it!

Steph Some were chucking their knickers!

Yvonne I didn't want to get up but they got me, didn't they?

Steph Two of 'em. One of them was that black one...

Yvonne God knows what I'm doing, then they spin me around about a dozen times. I didn't know what was going off. I'd already had four rum and cokes, so I was dizzy before I got up there. Anyway, so I'm oiling this other one, aren't I?

Steph You should've seen her!

Yvonne And I'm thinking, "Hallo", what are you doing? And then this big one grabs me, didn't he...

Steph You should've seen her dancing...

Yvonne I'm just up there, me, dancing with 'em. I couldn't get hold of them because they were that oily, it was like grabbing a bar of soap! Ooops, slipped out! Talk about laugh! (*She picks up a rabbit, looks at it and momentarily swings it as a penis*) Hey, this is good.

Steph Oh, nice.

Yvonne I don't like yours!

Steph Oh, he's nice.

Yvonne Yeah?

Steph Nice arse.

Yvonne Oh, yes!

Steph And you know what?

Yvonne What?

Steph He fucks like a rabbit!

Grant, Yvonne and Steph fall about laughing

Ron—Malvolio-like—emerges from the caravan half asleep and stands watching

Yvonne (*noticing Ron*) Here he is, another one. Go on, Ron, get 'em off. Show us what you've got and all. I'll do the music. Da, da, da, da... Come on! Show us your stomach muscles! (*She plays up to Ron*)

Ron I thought you weren't drinking.

Yvonne I've only had one.

Grant One too many.

Ron Come on, that's enough. Let's get you in bed.

Yvonne Yes, go on, go and get in that sleeping bag, so I can ravish you!

Steph See, told you, didn't I? Told you your luck was in!

Ron Yvonne?

Yvonne All that nylon, wonderful! Hey, Ron, if they zip us up together there'd be that much friction we'd set the bloody caravan on fire.

Ron What can you do when they're drunk?

Yvonne makes a drunken scene

Yvonne There he is, look, the man who kept Doncaster Highfields School open, against all the odds; the man who gave everything to the education system and it sent him round the bend. Oh, that's funny. You look really funny.

Ron Come on, let's have you.

Yvonne Let's have me? That'd be a turn up for the books!

Ron Yvonne?

Yvonne What a body?

Steph Oooh...

Yvonne Coooor! Just have a look at that, the sexiest man in the bloody world!
Ron Yes, very funny, very good!

All laugh, save Ron. Yvonne flings the rabbit to Ron who catches it

Yvonne Here, have a rabbit!

Yvonne bursts into laughter as do Steph and Grant. Ron is not amused

Music plays. The Lights fade to Black-out

END OF ACT I

ACT II

Scene 1

Early morning

The Lights come up on a very warm day

Ron is sorting his gas bottle out, it ran out during the night and he is making sure it will not gas them

Steph comes out, she is looking very sexy in a short denim skirt, white clogs and a skimpy top. She smokes

Steph Oh, hell, the morning after, again!
Ron Gas bottle!
Steph Run out?
Ron I forgot to turn the heating off. We were roasted during the night.
Steph How is she?
Ron Well, she's suffering now I've had this on. She's down by the sea, a bottle of aspirin in one hand and a glass of liver salts in the other.
Steph Not too well, then?
Ron She's felt better.
Steph Well, she was putting them away.
Ron Oh, she can do.
Steph For every one I had, she had two!
Ron Well, she's got three months catching up to do, hasn't she? (*He blows his nose*) Bloody hay fever.

Silence

Steph Grant's dead to the world. Mind you, he's like that most mornings.
Ron Thank him for the rabbit, by the way. (*He sneezes*) Ah, the grass, it gets me in the mornings.

A beat

Steph I'll tell you something, it was wild down there last night.

Ron Was it!

Steph But I think you've got to go crazy every now and again, don't you? Otherwise you'd go bloody mad!

Ron Maybe.

A beat

Steph So do you?

Ron What?

Steph Go mad?

Ron Not any more.

Steph Oh, boring!

Ron I just want to put my feet up and take it steady. And I've even gone the extra yard now I've bought that. It's a sure sign. (*Referring to the caravan*)

Steph Is it?

Ron You know when people buy cars they can be seen as penis extensions, can't they?

Steph Can they?

Ron Well, you know, look at me, I've got a big car.

Steph Have you?

Ron No, no, I haven't got a big car. I've got a family car.

Steph Well, it looks like a big car.

Ron Yes, it is a big car, but that's not the point. It's not a penis extension.

Steph Isn't it?

Ron No, it's just a big family car to pull the caravan. But the point is, now I've got a caravan, I've as much said, "look at me, I've opted out of the rat race, I've put my slippers under the awning". Well, actually, I couldn't get the awning up, so if that's a metaphor for anything I'm snookered.

A beat

Steph How old are you, then?

Ron Me? Nearly forty-four.

Steph Grant's that. And he's still got plenty of life left in him!

Ron Yes, but, what do they say. You're only as old as the woman you feel?

Steph Who says that, then?

Ron It's a saying!

Steph Oh, that's good that is. Mind you, if it works the other way around it doesn't say a lot for me, does it?

Ron No, I don't suppose it does.

Steph Anyway, you're happy enough, aren't you?

Ron Me?

Steph You wouldn't want to trade Yvonne in for another model, would you?

Ron Not with the same amount of mileage on anyway.

Steph I bet she was wild when she was younger!

Ron No, not really. She was quite quiet when we met. It's that bloody long ago now I can't remember to be honest. No, most of the time she's reliable old Yvonne.

Steph Well, she knows how to enjoy herself.

Ron Well, she likes a laugh, you know, like the rest of us.

Steph Not much. You've got a wild one there, I wouldn't let her out of my sight if I was you!

Ron Well, I don't think she'll get up to much this morning, not the way she was feeling at five o'clock.

Steph I know, I still feel a bit rough.

Silence

Ron So it sounds like it was a good night?

Steph It was a right scream.

Ron Did they do the full bit then, you know, the full bit?

Steph What?

Ron You know, all off?

Steph Oh, yeah!

Ron Oh, right.

Steph Oh ay, it all comes off.

Ron Oh, right.

Steph You can touch some of 'em if you're lucky enough. Mind you, what do you expect for seven quid?

Ron Oh, right.

Steph Why, were you thinking of doing it?

Ron Not me!

Steph There were a lot of seven quids in there last night. Somebody's making a packet!

Ron No, I'm too old for all that!

Steph I've always liked older men to be honest.

Ron Ah right!

Steph No, I think older men are a lot more sorted.

Ron Do you?

Steph Don't you?

Ron Well, I'm not.

Steph No, I do.

Ron Anyway, I don't think anyone would want to pay seven quid to see me get my kit off.

Steph Yvonne might.

Ron No.

Steph No?

Ron She's never liked parting with money at the best of times. I can't see her forking out seven quid for me to flash my bits.

Steph Not when she's seen most of 'em anyway!

Ron Most of 'em? How many do you think I've got?

Steph Well, you never know.

Ron No, my stripping days are definitely over.

Steph Oh, you see, boring.

Ron I showed my bum out of the back of a mini bus once.

Steph Oh, you devil!

Ron Must have been twenty years ago. I couldn't do it now, I'd probably get my arse stuck in the window or something.

A beat

Steph Well, I think you're sweet.

Ron Sweet?

Steph Yeah.

Ron That's about the least sexy thing you can ever say to a man.

Steph What, even a boring one?

Ron Anyway, I'd better get this gas bottle sorted.

Steph Oh, don't take it personal. It was only a joke, I'm only pulling your leg. I mean, Yvonne's a wild woman, you'd have to have sommat special to be able to cope with her, wouldn't you?

Ron Do you reckon?

Steph Oh ay, you'd have to be some kind of bloody nutcase! Anyway, I'll see you later. His Lordship wants a bacon sarnie bringing. Sometimes it makes you wonder if it's all worthwhile, doesn't it?

As Steph exits, Ron stops and watches her go

Ron Yes, it does, doesn't it?

Music. Black-out

Scene 2

Several hours later

A very weary Yvonne comes back from her walk

Ron stands where we left him. He looks at her as she gently lowers herself into a chair

Ron I thought you'd got lost!

Yvonne Oh, don't!

Ron Still bad?

Yvonne Not good!

Ron The brain shrinks when you drink too much.

Yvonne Well, you drink every day.

Ron Yeah, my brain's about the size of a pea. I expect to lose it one day down a nostril.

Yvonne Ohh, I feel rough.

Silence

Ron You won't fancy a bit of rabbit, then? I've skinned it and cooked it, I thought you might try an eyeball or something?

Yvonne Urghh!

Ron The fur took some getting off, but...

Yvonne Ron...?

Ron I've had the back two legs myself. Tasty!

Yvonne You haven't?

Ron I'm joking.

Yvonne What shall we do with it?

Ron I've stuck it in the fridge.

Yvonne Don't put it in the fridge! Bung it in the car boot!

Ron He might want the skin back, or a foot or something. You're going to have to eat it!

Yvonne Ron, I can't keep an aspirin down at the moment, so there is no way I'm going to eat a rabbit. Not now, not ever! I feel disgusted with myself as it is.

Ron I told you not to go.

Yvonne It not the stripping, it's the drink.

Ron So you had a good time, then?

Yvonne Actually, it was quite well done, quite professional. If you must know!

Ron Oh, come on!

Yvonne It was.

Ron Come on!

Yvonne What?

Ron No mention of dick size or bum quality?

Yvonne What are you on about?

Ron Just a modest, "It was quite well done"! What are you hiding?

Yvonne Nothing.

Ron "It was quite well done"?

Yvonne Oh, don't!

Ron "I liked the oiling down scene particularly, and I thoroughly enjoyed the bum massaging, but felt that the zip-pulling ballet was thin on substance. Over all, quite well done." Thank you, Yvonne Marlowe, theatre critic for the *Caravan Weekly*!

Yvonne It was actually a good show!

Ron Why don't you just tell me what it was really like?

Yvonne Go yourself, if you're so curious. I'll lend you a skirt!

Ron "It was quite well done"?

Yvonne It was professional.

Ron You don't mean to tell me that's what you were thinking, while you were watching it?

Yvonne I don't know what I was thinking.

Ron I suppose when it finished, one of them sang an aria for twenty minutes while the others danced about behind him?

Yvonne It was actually quite stylish. Why do you mock everything I do?

A beat

Ron Well, that's three months on the wagon, gone!

Yvonne I mean, I had to have a drink to get through it!

Ron Steph said you were putting them away.

Yvonne It is very hard to be stone cold sober in that kind of atmosphere! Anyway, you used to drink at the Amateurs. When we did *The Vagabond King* you were pissed most nights!

Ron I've rung the girls by the way, everything's fine.

Yvonne Did you tell them?

Ron What, that you'd got drunk, and seen The Flying Dicks?

Yvonne You're not going to let this drop, are you?

Ron Grant the grunt reckons they're all gay, but...

Yvonne What did you say?

Ron What could I say? "Your mother's gone native, all this marathon running, and health food is just a front, deep down she's really a raving voyeur"?

Yvonne Why do I bother?

Ron I told them you'd gone for a jog. Why, you're not ashamed of yourself, are you?

Yvonne Well, I shouldn't be, but you make me feel like I am.

A beat

Well, say something.

Ron Don't you worry about it. You're a well-educated, sensitive, attractive, highly sexual, married mother of three, who's stuck with a neurotic old fart.

Yvonne You said that!

Ron It's absolutely natural that you should want to go and watch six handsome young blokes parade their manhood, I mean who wouldn't?

Yvonne Sometimes!

Ron It's the animal button, isn't it? It's either on or off. And yours is obviously on. I suppose some people can never turn theirs off!

Yvonne You can.

Ron Well, I'm the exception, aren't I? I mean, we can't all be perfect.

Love-making noises can be heard coming from the caravan nearby

Steph Oh, oh, oh, oh, oh.

Ron Here we go! Just in time for the matinée.

Steph Oh, oh, oh!

Ron Early today, aren't they?

Yvonne It's too hot in there surely?

Ron You've got to admire their durability, haven't you? Three o'clock in the afternoon and the chocks are off. Everybody else is relaxing but not the Grunts!

Steph Oh oh.

Ron I might eat that rabbit myself when I think about it. It certainly works for him!

Yvonne Oh, hell.

Ron This is just... Isn't it bizarre, utterly ridiculous! Why does he have to do that? Does he think we can't hear?

Yvonne It's not him, is it, it's her.

Ron What do you mean?

Yvonne Well, she's making all the fuss.

Ron But he starts it off.

Yvonne What's wrong, are you jealous?

Ron I probably am, now you come to mention it!

Yvonne You are, aren't you?

Ron I'd never last the course, would I? Not with somebody like Steph. Be honest. I'd probably twist my back and come out bent double. I mean they must have detachable limbs or something. Because if I even try and make a cup of tea in ours I tie myself in knots!

Steph Oh oh...

Ron I can't sit here listening to this. I thought we might go out on a boat. They've refurbished the Hispaniola.

Yvonne Not a chance.

Ron It goes across the bay...

Yvonne I think I'm going to need some stronger tablets. Do we have any Nurofen? (*She gets up to go into the caravan*)

The noise from Steph changes tone

Steph No, Grant, no, please no, Grant! Grant, no…
Ron Oh, right!
Steph No no no … oh oh…
Yvonne Is she all right?
Ron How do I know?
Steph No, please…
Yvonne That sounds a bit…

A beat

    Why don't you go and find out?
Ron Find out what?
Yvonne What's going on.
Steph No, no, Grant, please…
Ron What am I going to do?
Yvonne Well, it sounds a bit…
Ron I know it sounds a bit…
Steph Please no … oh, oh!
Yvonne Ron, do something.
Ron What?
Yvonne I don't know!
Ron What if it's all part of it?
Yvonne All part of what?
Ron The thing?
Yvonne What thing?
Ron The animal thing?
Yvonne What are you on about?
Ron Oh, come on…!
Yvonne Ron, I've got a splitting head, I'm dying here, don't play twenty
    questions with me!
Ron What if it's a game?
Yvonne It doesn't sound like a game.
Ron But what if it is one?
Yvonne It sounds too real.
Ron What if they're playing, "slap me, slap me"?
Yvonne Eh?
Ron Slap me, slap me!
Yvonne What sort of bloody game is that?
Ron Oh, come on!
Yvonne Slap me, slap me?
Ron I say "no", but I mean "yes".

Steph Oh, oh, no...

Ron I mean, what if I suddenly storm in there and discover they're sat reading the papers and smoking.

Steph No, no. Grant, no, please, no. Oh.

Yvonne I think you should do something!

Ron You do something.

Yvonne Like what?

Ron Throw some water over them or something. That's what my dad used to do with the dog.

Yvonne Oh God, I feel awful.

Ron I suppose we could go.

Yvonne Eh?

Ron We could just go.

Yvonne Why?

Steph Oh, oh, oh!

Ron That's why! That's what's great about having a caravan, you go to one place, and if you don't like it you go somewhere else.

Yvonne We can't go, it looks bad.

Ron And this doesn't look bad, living next door to Fred and Wilma Flintstone?

Yvonne I thought they were all right. I thought you could cope with them because you were from the same background, what happened to all that?

Ron walks across the pitch and shouts

Ron Hallo?

Yvonne Ron?

Ron Hallo! We can hear you. We know what you're doing!

Steph Oh, oh, oh! No...

Ron (*shouting*) Shut up, for God's sake, give it a bloody rest!

Yvonne Ron, stop shouting, please!

Ron I can't believe this.

Yvonne I can't go anywhere, I feel so awful!

Steph Oh, oh! Oh...

The noise stops

Yvonne They've stopped.

Ron Only to refuel.

Yvonne Oh, my bloody head!

Ron I never saw it like this. I'd got it down as seagulls squawking and the smell of cow shit.

Yvonne The man's a pig.

Ron I don't know about you, but my imagination is working over time.

Yvonne Do you think we should do something?

Ron Like what?

Yvonne Well, report them.

Ron Who to?

Yvonne Well, the site warden or somebody, call the police. Just as a precaution.

Ron Report them what for?

Yvonne Well…

Ron Yes, "Hallo, is that the police, well, we've heard some aggressive love-making going on in the next caravan, and we don't think it's normal." "Well, what were you doing listening, sir? Haven't you got anything better to do?"

Yvonne I mean, you never know, do you?

Ron Well, no, you don't, but…

Yvonne He treats her like she's one of his bloody dogs or something. I've a good mind to say something to him.

Ron Don't say a word, for God's sake.

Yvonne If you ever did that sort of thing to me I'd leave you.

Ron What sort of thing?

Yvonne Well, whatever's making her shout like that!

Ron If I ever did that sort of thing to you, love, I'd need a back-up team!

Yvonne walks towards the other caravan

Yvonne Don't be bloody funny!

Ron Where are you going? Come away. Leave it be!

Yvonne I think she puts some of that on, you know? She must know we can hear!

Ron So who's she putting it on for?

Yvonne Well, it's not me.

Ron Well, it's not for me, is it?

Yvonne I don't know.

Ron It's obviously for the grunt, isn't it?

Yvonne Oh, listen. I think they're starting again.

Ron Oh, I'm going, I can't stand another bout of that. (*He is about to lift the gas bottle*)

Yvonne Where are you going?

Ron I'm going to refill the gas bottle.

Yvonne Ron, it's absolutely boiling, we don't need the heating on.

Ron No, but after all that thrashing about, I need a strong cup of tea. Besides, this looks like the only exercise I'll be getting this holiday!

Music. Black-out

SCENE 3

Later that afternoon

Grant comes out of the caravan. He has a large bowl of potato peelings

As he walks out, Steph comes to him with some empty cans of beans, and a carrier bag

Steph Here, take the rest of the rabbit giblets!
Grant Leave that foot that I've left on the sink, I want to make our Josh a key ring.
Steph You've forgotten half the bloody rubbish. Why are you so useless?
Grant Thought you'd finished!
Steph And look at me eye, I'm going to have a right shiner there.
Grant It'll be right.
Steph It will. I'll look a right fuckin' mess.
Grant It wa' an accident.

A beat

Steph Are they about?
Grant He's gone a walk, don't know where she is.
Steph Ron says she felt like shit.
Grant Oh dear!
Steph I was thinking. They've got some nice stuff, haven't they?
Grant Ay, we'll have some of that.

Steph looks at Ron's and Yvonne's chairs

Steph Nice chairs, mind you, they're mucky to say they're new.
Grant And I tell you sommat else.
Steph What?
Grant She's got mucky knickers.
Steph You what?
Grant Her knickers are filthy. I'd chuck most of 'em out if I was her.
Steph Since when have you seen her knickers?
Grant She wants to get some new 'uns. Typical of that type, they come all the new caravan and their knickers are hung on the line, falling to bloody bits. I wouldn't let you wear what she wears.
Steph She's all right!
Grant I'm not saying she in't. She likes a drink and a laugh, and that's fair enough. But I don't think she has much fun wi' him, does she? (*He inspects Ron's caravan. He looks at the lock on the hitch*) Nice caravan though.

Steph He's all right.

Grant He's a fart.

Steph Oh God, sometimes!

Grant Look at that, they've got the top of the range lock on it and all. Bloody hell. See! They must have some money! Top of the range lock. Sixteen quid that. You can get one for four pound. I mean, why put a top of the range lock on? It's all for bloody show!

Steph They're all right, a bit starchy, but ... she's a laugh really!

Grant looks at the caravan on stage

Grant Fourteen grand?

Steph Nice.

Grant Never worth that.

Steph Nice though.

Grant You lose three grand the minute you put it on a site.

Steph You lose another three when we pull up.

Grant You bloody do and all! Mind you, that's a good van. I know it's had some stick, but it's as good a van as there is on this site!

Steph I could live with that no trouble.

Grant Needs an awning on it to finish it off, though.

Steph She told me he's useless, couldn't put it up.

Grant Bloody easy.

Steph Couldn't do it, though, not without the instructions. She said he has to have the instructions for everything or he's hopeless.

Grant I thought he was a bloody headmaster. Thought he was supposed to be bloody genius or sommat.

Steph Do you want any peas with this or what?

Grant looks in Ron's caravan

Grant Yeah. I'll have some peas. Hey, they've got all fancy stuff in here, look!

Steph Are you going to take that rubbish?

Grant Ar.

Steph starts to go back to her caravan. As she does, Grant has a look around Ron's caravan and then sees their waste bin and puts his rubbish in their waste bin

Steph Don't do that, you ignorant get!

Grant Fuck 'em! (*He bursts into laughter*)

Steph looks at him and laughs as well

Steph You bloody idiot!

Music. Black-out

SCENE 4

Later

Grant is sitting relaxing in one of his chairs, he has a can of beer

Yvonne enters after having just been for a jog. She is sweating heavily

Yvonne Oh! I sometimes wonder if it's all worthwhile.
Grant Looks like horse work!
Yvonne I thought it might clear my head.
Grant (*referring to the beer bottle*) This clears mine.
Yvonne I think I feel worse.
Grant It's too warm, isn't it?
Yvonne It is now, I'm boiling. (*She peels off her jogging top revealing figure-hugging sports gear. She has been sweating*)

Grant looks at her. We see the shape of her torso. Patches of sweat

Grant Ay, it's warm today.
Yvonne It is after six miles.
Grant Worked up a sweat, then?
Yvonne Yes, I needed to.
Grant Ay, looks like you've worked up a sweat. I like a good sweat.
Yvonne You'll not sweat much doing that.
Grant Oh, I dunno. Anyway, I've done my sweating for today.

Yvonne reclines and gets her breath back

Yvonne (*breathless*) Really?
Grant I like feeling it run down my face.
Yvonne (*tired*) Oh, dear!
Grant She says you're running the marathon?
Yvonne Hoping to.
Grant Must be fit, then?
Yvonne What?
Grant Must be fit for that?
Yvonne I don't feel it today.

Grant I don't fancy it myself.
Yvonne Well...
Grant I reckon it's boring.
Yvonne It is. You have to go through things in your head. It helps me work things out.
Grant I've seen it on the telly, but...
Yvonne I watched it last year and wanted to do something different.

A beat

Grant Like doing things that are different, do you?
Yvonne Well...
Grant You like doing different things, then?
Yvonne Within reason.
Grant Makes a change I bet.
Yvonne I think I'd draw the line at parachuting. I don't think Ron would like it much anyway.
Grant Keeps you on a short lead, does he?
Yvonne Sorry?
Grant I say, he likes to keep his eye on you?
Yvonne Well.
Grant See what you're up to?
Yvonne Not really.
Grant So he's not bothered what you do, then?
Yvonne Well...
Grant I think you've got to keep an eye on 'em all the time. I have her. She's a right bloody headcase.
Yvonne She is, she led me astray.
Grant Oh!
Yvonne Yes, I'm afraid.
Grant Oh!
Yvonne What?
Grant That's not what she said.
Yvonne No?
Grant Oh, no.
Yvonne Well, there you go.

A beat

Grant Mind you, I've got dogs like that, you know?
Yvonne Like what?
Grant That you can't let loose?
Yvonne Yes, I bet you have!

Grant You've got to keep a fuckin' chain on 'em or they'd be off sniffin' around any old bitch.
Yvonne I'm sure.

A beat

Grant You had your rabbit yet?
Yvonne Not yet.
Grant You want to get it eaten before it turns. Has he ever skinned one before?
Yvonne I wouldn't have thought so.
Grant I'll come and do it for you if you want. If he doesn't know how to do it!
Yvonne Well, let's see how he gets on!

A beat

Grant Steph said it was a good night?
Yvonne Oh, that?
Grant (*laughing*) Ah?
Yvonne What?
Grant Bloody women!
Yvonne What about us?
Grant You're all the same.
Yvonne You think so?
Grant Argh dear!
Yvonne What?
Grant I mean, I'm not against it. We've had it our way for long enough, haven't we?
Yvonne Yes, I think you have.
Grant Mind you, she said you went for it!
Yvonne Anyway...!
Grant Trying to forget about it, eh?
Yvonne Trying to.
Grant It's only human nature, in't it, it's like I told her... Nowt to be ashamed on.
Yvonne I'd better get a shower and... (*She moves towards her caravan*)
Grant Ay, she said that they were baying for blood down there last night. Mind you, I says, that's what it's for, in't it, them as not getting any.
Yvonne It was a good night actually!
Grant I says, she'll not want to go and see them strippers but when she gets there she'll probably go bloody loopy!
Yvonne Well...?

Grant It happens wi't dogs. You chain 'em up for that long, when you let 'em off they'd bloody kill you if they got you.

Yvonne Right.

Grant They'd never get me, though, I'm too quick for 'em!

Yvonne It was a good night. The pizza was a bit of a let down but we had quite a laugh.

Grant Ay, but she said that you were well out of order!

Yvonne She said that, did she?

Grant I said, bloody typical.

Yvonne Actually...

Grant Oh ay, trying to get out of it now, are you?

Yvonne Wait till I see her.

Grant stands with his drink, finishes it off

Grant Anyway, I'd better get some ale in. You don't want owt bringing, do you? Or has he put the mockers on you having any more?

Yvonne I don't feel like any at the moment.

Grant You should see her in there, she can sup more than me, and that's saying something.

Yvonne Now, I don't believe that for one minute.

Grant It's right!

Yvonne I think I've had enough to last me a whole year.

Grant Arh, can't trust yourself, eh?

Yvonne I don't like being out of control...

Grant Just like her in there, when she's had a few drinks she's absolutely anybody's.

Yvonne Well, I wouldn't go that far!

Grant I've got to watch her like a fuckin' hawk sometimes!

Grant exits

Yvonne watches, as he goes

Music. Black-out

SCENE 5

Later, evening

The Lights come up on Yvonne in the caravan, Ron facing her. It is quite dim inside. He is making some sandwiches

Ron Well, what do you expect from him, Shakespeare's sonnets?

Yvonne He's so…

Ron What?

Yvonne Brutal!

Ron The man breeds bull-terriers, you're not going to get any coffee morning banter from him, are you?

Yvonne He's got the social skills of a slug, honestly!

Ron Well, dogs don't talk a lot unless you hadn't noticed.

Yvonne It's the way he looks at you and grunts.

Ron Ham or cheese?

Yvonne Ham.

Ron continues making tea

Ron There was a lad at school like him, he used to scare me to bloody death.

Yvonne He sits there with his belly, urgh dear!

Ron He made my life a misery. Danny Ward. Big Danny Ward. God, he was rough. Rough as a bear's arse. I think he was shaving when he was ten. Every day he took my dinner tickets, every day for five years. I never thought of it as bullying at the time, but I suppose it was really. God knows what he did with them, he must have had thousands of my bloody dinner tickets!

Yvonne He keeps going on about last night. He's so bloody thick, obviously can't cope with it, and he's got nothing else to talk about.

Ron He's all right really.

Yvonne God knows what she told him. It's the way he looks at you; (*as Grant*) "Seen them strippers ooh". He's like a cartoon.

Ron The country's full of men like him, Yvonne, they're called people. You need to get out more!

Yvonne And they always seem to be attracted to me. And what she's doing with him, I just don't know! I mean, she's really naïve, and sweet and…

Ron She's great, I told you. (*He hands a sandwich to Yvonne*)

Yvonne What does she see in him even?

Ron Well, he's obviously good at one thing, isn't he? And I don't think they teach that at school.

Yvonne No, if they had done, I suspect you would have studied it to degree level.

Ron Well, A level at least!

Yvonne She was telling me about what they get up to.

Ron Oh, right.

Yvonne Very frank and open.

Ron Don't tell me, it'll only depress me.

Yvonne How could she possibly sleep with him. He's such a pig. And he's done that twice now!

Ron Done what?

Yvonne Been hanging about.

Ron Well, what do you want him to do? We're almost sleeping together, aren't we? Is he out there by the way? (*He looks out of the window*)

Yvonne No, he's gone to swing on the tyres I think.

Ron Oh, we shouldn't mock him really.

Yvonne It's just how he is always floating about.

Ron Well, we're sharing a pitch, kid. What do you want me to say, "stop talking to my wife", she's reading all sorts into it.

Yvonne You don't have to read into it.

Ron That's what passes for badinage, that's the banter of the workplace! Didn't you do Bernstein's language codes at Oxford?

Yvonne Not on the Music course.

Ron Welcome to the real world.

A beat

Yvonne (*with a mouthful of bread*) So you don't think we should do anything about it?

Ron Anything about what?

Yvonne About all that noise.

Ron There's nothing that needs doing, is there?

Yvonne Well, no, except for the fact that there is a man across the way who is knocking a woman about...

Ron We don't know that!

Yvonne Well, he's using insinuating behaviour...

Ron Yvonne, lighten up, we're on a caravan site.

A beat

Yvonne Well, I think that we should go.

Ron Are you serious?

Yvonne Yes, I am. We've had a trial, haven't we? I mean, we've worked out how everything works.

Ron Yes, but...?

Yvonne I'd like to get home to be honest.

Ron Why, do you still feel hung over?

Yvonne Well, I don't feel brilliant.

Ron Oh, great, you make a fool of yourself and we've got to go home!

Yvonne Well, I can't say I'm enjoying it, can you?

Ron Yes, it's fine!

Yvonne Well, I'm not.

Ron You were loving it before Steph and Grant pulled up!

Yvonne It was all right.

Ron Well, we might as well sell the soddin' thing then.

Yvonne Why are you always so extreme?

Ron Fourteen grand down the bloody pan. What do you think we'll get for it? We'd be lucky to get ten. Ten grand and we've slept in it once.

Yvonne I didn't say we should sell it. I just think we should be more choosy with the sites.

Ron It was last minute, you know it was. All the Caravan Club sites were booked up.

Yvonne Well, we should try one of them, I mean this is just a field, isn't it?

Ron They are all just fields!

Yvonne Yes, but…

Ron I mean, I can't help it if you feel humiliated about last night.

Yvonne I don't feel humiliated.

A beat

Ron Well, I suppose we'll just have to go in the morning then. Jeez…!

Yvonne We can see if there's any vacancies on the way back.

Ron It'll probably take me four days to pack the bloody car up again. I'm just going to load everything in the van and that's it. I'm not listing everything, it's a waste of time. Meanwhile, don't go hanging your knickers on the clothes line.

Yvonne What are you saying, that I'm leading him on?

Ron No!

Yvonne Yes!

Ron No!

Yvonne That's what you're saying.

Ron I'm not saying that.

Yvonne Yes, you are.

Ron Well, it might have helped if you hadn't given him the full story and started swinging the rabbit about. You could see he was getting off on it!

Yvonne You come out with such rubbish at times for an educated man.

Ron And you do some bloody silly things for an educated woman.

Yvonne You never support me, do you?

Ron I'm not getting into it. You want to go tomorrow, we'll go tomorrow, I don't want to get into the rights or wrongs of what's gone off, I want to forget it.

Yvonne You never do, you never do anything to support me.

Ron What do you want me to do, go and give the grunt a good hiding?

Yvonne You've never done that yet.

Ron You want the bloody good hiding if anybody.

Yvonne Oh, grow up, little boy!

Ron I'm a little boy? You've been caught playing naughty and you want to go home. Ah, dear me!

Yvonne You don't know what it's like having somebody look at you all the time! He just looks at me, I could slap him I could!

Ron Yes, we're both agreed, the man's a bloody animal, for God's sake. So why don't you go over and wallop him, you're the one doing all the training!

Yvonne I might.

Ron Oh, very good.

Yvonne I might do yet.

Ron In fact, why don't you go over and ask him for a session because that's what you're really after!

Silence

Yvonne What?

Ron That's what it all seems like to me!

Yvonne Oh, you are just pathetic sometimes, do you know that?

Yvonne storms out of the caravan and exits

Ron Yes, love, you tell me every day!

Music. Black-out

SCENE 6

An hour later

Steph comes from her caravan with some food remnants. She now has a decent black eye. Ron is packing up the awning as she comes out

Steph Hiya!

Ron Oh, hiya! Just sorting this out. Lost without the instructions.

Steph She feeling any better?

Ron Yes, I think so, she's had a jog, sweated some of it out.

Steph Yeah, Grant said he'd had a nice little chat!

Ron Have you taken a bang?

Steph Eh?

Ron Your eye...?

Steph Accident.

Ron Right.

Steph You know what it's like, can't swing a cat...

Ron I wondered because we heard some shouting earlier, but...

Steph Sorry about that.

Ron No problem, as long as everything's OK.

Steph Did you hear?

Ron I think they heard you in Newcastle to be honest.

Steph Shit!

Ron In fact, I think they could pick some of it up in Holland.

Steph Have I gone red?

Ron No, but I did.

Steph It's Grant, he's bloody crackers...

Ron Is he about?

Steph He's gone to the site next door. It's talent night, so he's trying to get me booked in. I'm doing Cher, *Gypsies, Tramps and Thieves*.

Ron Oh, right. Great!

Steph We're not supposed to go into the club, but Grant knows somebody. I won thirty quid one weekend.

Ron Really?

Steph Yeah, I know, not bad, is it?

Grant comes on to the pitch. He has a large cardboard crate of beer with him

Grant Come on, woman, put the bloody kettle on! Don't just stand there!

Steph Listen to him... Who does he think he is?

Grant Look at this, twenty-five quid for this lot. Ronnie said they'd fallen off the back of a warehouse.

Steph Have you booked me on?

Grant Quarter to nine. You're on after some twat doing Buddy Holly. And some kids doing Boyzone!

Steph Oh, there's always Buddy Holly.

Steph goes inside the caravan

Grant She's doing Cher.

Ron She said.

Grant *Gypsies, Tramps and Thieves*. I mean, it's thirty quid a pop, not bad you know, nearly pay for a week up here.

Ron That's right.

Grant I like it when she does Kate Bush the best... "Oh, me, I'm Cathy, I'm coming home." Whatever the fuck it is.

Ron Sounds good!

Grant You ought to get Yvonne across, if she's a bit of a singer.

Ron Yes, that's right.
Grant See how good she is. Who could she do?
Ron No idea.
Grant She couldn't do Cilla Black, could she?
Ron No, I don't think she's right for that.
Grant And she's not Tina Turner, is she?
Ron No. Lesley Garratt?
Grant Lulu.
Ron Lulu?
Grant I tell you what...
Ron Go on...
Grant Dusty Springfield!
Ron You reckon?
Grant Oh ay, she's a spit!
Ron Yes, now you come to mention it...
Grant Easy, she's easily Dusty Springfield, in't she, or Bonnie Tyler? She
    might even away with Blondie!
Ron Yeah?

Grant sings, badly, "I Just Don't Know What To Do With Myself"

    That's right.
Grant Good song that...

Ron sings, badly, another line from the song

    I just don't know what to do... That's right.
Ron That's right.

Both men join in a fairly poor few lines of the song

Ron I don't think we should enter.
Grant Oh, us, no chance, but she's easily Dusty Springfield, in't she? I mean,
    she's got the gob, an't she?
Ron That's right.

A beat

Grant I can't handle the bloody heat to be honest. Are you having one? (*He
    tears a beer from the crate*)
Ron Not for me.
Grant Mention it to her, then we can come back and have a few! Get a barbie
    going maybe...
Ron That'd be good...

Grant I can get some more rabbits if you want.

Ron Well, I think we can manage at the moment, thanks.

Grant It's funny her doing singing and all, in't it?

Ron Eh?

Grant Yvonne and Steph both of 'em, are into singing?

Ron Oh, yes!

Grant But Yvonne's funny, in't she, when she's had a few. When she was playing with that rabbit! Funny!

Ron It was, wasn't it?

Grant I'd like to see her up there. I'd like to see if she can put it over, you know, because she's got it all, hasn't she, all the attitude?

Ron That's right...

Grant Well, I'd better help her get ready, or I'll be getting a black eye. (*He picks up his baggage and makes to exit. Suddenly he spins and stops*) Tell her I'll give her a knock. Dusty Springfield, you tell her!

Ron I will.

Grant Hey, I've just had a thought.

Ron What?

Grant You never know, she might even get away with Petula Clarke!

Grant exits

Ron goes back to the awning

Music. Black-out

SCENE 7

Half an hour later

Ron and Yvonne are outside their caravan. Ron is laughing and animated. Yvonne is preparing to tidy away their garden furniture

Ron Oh, be fair!

Yvonne (*moderately loudly*) I'm not going!

Ron Keep your voice down.

Yvonne Just go and tell him we're busy.

Ron You tell him!

Yvonne What's wrong, are you scared?

Ron He's invited us out.

Yvonne To a talent night on the site next door? It's my complete *bête noire*!

Ron We've got to go.

Yvonne You go if you're so keen.

Ron Oh, we've got to go.

Yvonne I can't bear things like that, they're so tacky.

Ron You went to that one on the cruise, you enjoyed that!

Yvonne It was on the Orianna, for goodness sake!

Ron Well, you tell the grunt that!

Yvonne Oh, no, Ron, I can't go, no way. Anyway, we've got to pack. Tell him that. Tell him I'm not so well.

Ron You'll have to go because your mate's giving her Cher.

Yvonne What?

Ron Steph's doing Cher.

Yvonne Oh my God!

Ron Early stuff...

Yvonne Oh, hell... I can just imagine it.

Ron *Gypsies, Tramps and Thieves.*

Yvonne Oh, no, I can't bear it! I bet it's awful.

Ron And then he wants us to come back and have a barbecue...

Yvonne No, Ron, no!

Ron He's bought a crate.

Yvonne No!

Ron It gets better.

Yvonne It can't possibly get any worse, that's for sure.

Ron He wants you to enter the talent contest.

Yvonne No!

Ron That's what he says.

Yvonne No!

Ron He's going to come and give you a knock.

Yvonne No!

Ron Oh, you can't do this, this is what caravanning is all about.

Yvonne I am not singing.

Ron You've got to. He thinks you're having a good time.

Yvonne How wrong he is!

Ron Obviously it was the rabbit swinging that impressed him!

Yvonne There is no way I am going, now you can tell him or I will.

A beat

Ron Well, he reckons you could do a good Dusty Springfield.

Yvonne Don't be bloody ridiculous!

Ron I'm not being, he thinks you'd get away with Dusty Springfield.

Yvonne Dusty Springfield?

Ron Or Blondie at a push!

Yvonne One of you is mad!

Ron We've just been stood here singing the bloody lyrics.

Yvonne I'm not doing it! Forget Dusty Springfield.

Ron laughs

Ron All right, all right. What about Petula Clarke, then?
Yvonne You're serious, aren't you?

Ron trees to cajole Yvonne

Ron Oh, laugh!
Yvonne Why?
Ron Laugh at it.
Yvonne I can't!
Ron Laugh at it, Yvonne.
Yvonne Why, it's not funny. It's bloody tragic. It's a nightmare.
Ron It bloody is.
Yvonne I am not singing in a talent competition on a caravan site, no way, never ever! I'd rather die. I'd rather run through the streets naked. I'd rather be hung, drawn and quartered. No, no, no!

Silence

Ron Oh, go on, I'll buy you a drink! (*He laughs uproariously*)

Yvonne has to smile

Music. Black-out

Scene 8

Three hours later

Ron and Yvonne remain on stage, they are given drinks by the other two actors entering. Steph, who is dressed in a short black skirt with a moderate attempt at Cher, smokes and looks at the coast

A large number of crisps, hot dogs, empty cans of cheap beer and sandwiches are on stage. The barbecue has just come to an end. Its embers still glow

Grant enters with some more cans of beer

Everyone has had a bit too much to drink already. Grant offers a can of beer to Yvonne

Grant Here you are, Yvonne, have another, there's plenty more where that came from! I know you like a drink, lass!

Yvonne This is my last.

Grant Famous last words! You'll not be running many marathons on that.

Yvonne Not tonight anyway!

Grant There's some more pork chops if anybody's interested. She always buys too much, don't you, cock?

Steph Do I?

Grant Nice burgers! I got 'em off a bloke at the club, he buys 'em for the site. The thing about barbecues is, if you cook it too long, you burn it, and if you under cook it, everybody gets the shits, don't you reckon, Yvonne?

Yvonne That's right!

Ron I thought you did a good job. I try but I make a real mess of it. That's another thing I'm not very good at.

Yvonne Ron's OK if you like your food very, very burnt!

Grant You all right, Steph?

Steph Yeah!

A beat

Grant Well, I was impressed, weren't you, Steph?

Steph Yeah!

Grant Yes, I was impressed. Very good, Yvonne. Don't you think, cock?

Steph Not bad!

Grant She's got the fuckin' mood on because she didn't win.

Steph I haven't!

Grant She can't win every time, can she, Ron?

Ron No, but I thought she was terrific.

Steph I wasn't!

Grant Steph, Yvonne's studied singing, hasn't she, you slack get! She's bound to be bloody good.

Yvonne I don't think studying it...

Grant Shut up a minute, you, she's got to be told... She's like this every time sommat doesn't go her way. If you're not pleasing her, she's a bloody pain.

Ron I thought Steph did well...

Grant She did, I'm not saying she didn't, only you can tell class, can't you?

Ron Well, Yvonne's done a lot, you see...

Grant Mind you, you let me down, Yvonne. I wish you'd have done Dusty Springfield.

Yvonne It's not my——

Grant Shirley Bassey's all right though. (*He sings from* Goldfinger) Do it again.

Yvonne No, I——

Grant sings from Goldfinger

Very good!

Ron Excellent!

Grant (*singing*) "Goldfingaaar!"

Yvonne You've got it.

Grant Hey, Steph, what do you think, "Goldfingaaar"... Do you think I'd win?

Steph No.

Yvonne You've got the mouth for it anyway.

Grant Now I have got a gob on me! Hey, at least you didn't do any of that classical stuff. I thought when you got up there. I thought for God's sake don't do any classical stuff, some of them in that club are right bloody philistines.

Yvonne That's what I thought.

Ron I thought it was quite pleasant.

Grant Bloody heathens some of them. Pigs!

Steph Grant!

A beat

Grant So, go on then, what did you think of the talent?

Yvonne Well...

Grant Go on...

Yvonne Pretty average.

Ron Yvonne?

Yvonne Pretty average really.

Grant Really?

Yvonne In fact I thought some of it was dreadful to be honest.

Steph Oh, right!

Yvonne Well, Buddy Holly looked more like John Major for a start.

Ron Yvonne!

Yvonne Well, he couldn't sing, and he couldn't play guitar, which is a bit of a drawback if you're trying to be Buddy Holly!

Ron I thought he was all right.

Yvonne I thought that the atmosphere in the club was awful. Half of the audience weren't listening, they were just sat like they always are, presumably, waiting for the next game of bingo. And if the organist had hit the right notes once it would have been a miracle.

Ron Oh come on, be fair...

Yvonne I thought the kids who did "Boyzone" were backward, to be honest, and the woman who sang that song from *Titanic* was ill, you could see she was.

Ron Yvonne, be fair, they were just people who'd volunteered to get up, I mean...

Yvonne Yes, but why? What was the point of it?

Ron Well...

Yvonne Utter rubbish, the whole event...

Ron I don't understand you at times ... it was all right, Grant.

Yvonne By what criterion was it all right?

Ron It was people just having a go at something.

Yvonne Marks for effort rather than ability. Dumbing down.

Ron Not necessarily...

Grant Shut up a minute, you!

Ron I was all right, Steph...

Grant No, she's right, I thought it was shit to be honest. Wasn't it, Steph?

Steph I thought it was all right...

Ron I thought it was...

Grant Usually, there's one or two good singers but it was awful this weekend...

Steph is childishly hurt. She is becoming petulant

Steph I thought "Boyzone" were good. I mean they haven't had any training or owt, have they? It's not as if they're professionals or owt. It was just sommat to do. I don't know why you've had to rip 'em all to bits?

Yvonne Well, the grunt asked me my opinion, and now nobody likes it.

Ron Yvonne...!

Yvonne I can't do what you do, I can't pretend things are better than they are, you should know that!

Grant goes to grab Steph. She doesn't like it

Grant Steph, come and sit down, you're bugging me to bloody death standing up there, you're like a fuckin' lost woman.

Steph I'm all right!

Grant (*in a vicious temper*) I said come and sit down and have a fuckin' drink or sommat.

Yvonne I thought Steph was all right, actually.

Ron I thought she did really well...

Yvonne Honestly!

Steph I thought you said it was awful?

Yvonne I thought you were quite good ... good range, not bad at all...

Grant She was fuckin' rubbish, she missed half the bloody words.

Ron I thought you were great, really good.

Grant Don't patronize her, man, she was shite and she knows she was.

A beat

Ron Well, I thought you were good.
Grant She's usually a lot better than that rubbish.
Yvonne It is nerve wracking…

Steph is very brittle

Steph I got nervous. Put me off. It's wi' him being a teacher. I've never liked teachers, they're always judging you!
Ron No, I wasn't, I thought you were great!

A beat

Grant So what did they finish you for, then, Ron?
Ron Oh, dear…
Grant I got finished at pit after t' strike. Thirteen thousand, what a fucking joke, eh? Not even get me a caravan like yours.
Ron My nerves.
Grant They can finish you for that, can they?
Ron Well, they did me. I needed to get out.
Grant Thirteen thousand!
Ron I spent every day sorting out problems.
Grant Pressure job, you see…
Ron I never went in a classroom.
Grant Bit of a drawback for a teacher, then!
Ron Bloody staff having breakdowns, kids having breakdowns, pregnancies, bloody hell, you name it!
Grant Sounds like the school I went to… I was a bastard at school, Yvonne, I've calmed down now a bit!
Ron Then we had an inspection. That was fun!
Grant Always felt they were looking down on me at school, you know?
Ron Most of the kids were from broken homes…
Grant Better off now, though, eh?
Ron We were bottom of the league table!
Grant No more of that now, Ron…
Ron We couldn't get any parent governors!
Grant I told her, I'm glad they finished me. I spent six years getting over the bloody strike but I was glad to get out of the pit. I never thought I'd say that, but…
Ron Bloody nightmare…
Grant Five years in the bloody wilderness, man! Then I met Steph, didn't I? Best thing in my life!
Ron Smashing…
Grant Two years in March, in't it?

Steph Two year, in March...

Grant Married twice, won't I?

Steph Ay, he's that thick he made the same mistake, twice.

Grant Shut up, you witch! Three kids, you know? Great, aren't they, we bring 'em up here some weekends, don't we?

Steph He was on his own for three years, weren't you?

Grant She's brilliant with 'em, she is. Wayne my eldest is seventeen now, you should see him and her, they're like brother and sister, are you?

Steph He's a big 'un, in't he?

Grant Oh ay, he's a big 'un, he'd've made your nerves bad sorting him out, Ron.

Ron laughs. A thin veneer covers the dialogue

Ron We've got three, you know...

Grant Three girls? Oh, bloody hell, I couldn't handle it. Just think what they'll get up to when they're older. Just think what men'll want to do to 'em? No. I couldn't handle that.

Ron Well, I don't...

Grant If anybody touched my little girls I'd slit their throats. Men are bastards!

Ron I know.

Grant Bastards! Our Wayne is, in't he?

Steph He's a big 'un, in't he?

Grant Mind you some women are too, to think on it!

A beat

Yvonne Why did you get divorced, then?

Grant I didn't have a relationship, love. You know what I mean?

Steph It was awful, wasn't it?

Grant Awful! Killing me, wasn't she?

Steph Killing him, wasn't she?

Grant I kid you not, Ron, but everything I did for Denise was bloody wrong for her!

Ron Really?

Grant Everything! I couldn't put a foot right. We'd had three kids and everything I did for that bloody woman was wrong. I wish they'd've retired me from that marriage, talk about being bad with your nerves? And the other one before her, dopey Vicky, well, she was as soft as a brush. Bloody lesbian or sommat I think.

Yvonne You didn't have any kids to her, then?

Grant Are you joking, I couldn't get bloody near her... The day I met Steph was the best day of my life, wasn't it?

Ron Smashing…

Grant Now is everybody all right for a drink, Yvonne?

Yvonne No, I'm taking it steady.

Grant She dun't want a repeat performance of last night, does she?

Steph No wonder.

Grant Did she tell you what happened?

Ron Oh, yes!

Grant What a carry on. You know that she got up with 'em and all!

Ron No?

Grant Oh ay, she's a right one is this one, she was up with 'em dancing and rubbing oil in 'em, weren't you?

Steph Tell everybody…

Grant Oh ay, she likes to get her money's worth. I tell you, she's a right 'un when she's out. Mind you, did she tell you what she got up to?

Yvonne Ron knows all about it.

Grant Funny, eh?

Ron That's right.

Grant I mean, it's only a bit of fun though, isn't it? What a pair, I ask you, and they're as different again, aren't they?

Ron They are.

Grant But she's a maniac according to Steph. I don't know how you cope with her. Did she tell you what she let them do?

Ron No.

Yvonne We needn't get into all the detail, need we?

Grant I think it's hilarious, me, they didn't do it to Steph, but fancy letting 'em stuff your head down their trousers and waggle their wedding tackle in her face? I mean bloody funny! She didn't do it. But Steph said Yvonne did it twice. Must have liked it, Ron.

Ron Must have.

Grant Bloody funny.

Ron is ashen

I bet she got a bloody eyeful then, mate!

Ron I bet she did.

Grant Get down, have a look at that! Bloody hell, Yvonne, you make me laugh.

Yvonne (*light, laughing*) Well, you know…

Grant They both went backstage. God knows what for, couldn't get enough. Set of bloody queers. I think it's funny I do. She's a funny bugger is Yvonne, she's all prim and proper but when she's had a drink…

Yvonne That's me!

Grant Come here, you… (*He grabs Steph kindly*) She's lovely, in't she, in't she lovely?

Steph Am I?

Grant Well, are we going to call that a night then, sweetheart?

Steph Can do.

Grant Anyway, there's plenty of ale left if you want one.

Ron Right!

Grant I think Yvonne should take it steady, though, I don't want anybody on the site raping!

Yvonne (*trying to keep it light*) It's her, she's a bad influence on me.

Grant Anyway, good night, love. I thought you were brilliant up there, we'll do sommat tomorrow if you want! (*He kisses Yvonne. It is a long kiss and he feels the cup of her breast*)

Ron watches

Good-night. I've right enjoyed your company. Hey, take it steady if your nerves are bad, mate, my brother-in-law's nerves were all over the shop and he ended up gassing his fuckin' sen, didn't he?

Steph Awful!

Grant Come on, then...

Grant and Steph exit to their caravan

Yvonne and Ron sit and look at each other. Ron takes a few sips on his drink

Yvonne Shall we get cleared away, then? Be good to get off early...

Silence

What?

Ron Thank you.

Yvonne For what?

Ron For what?

Yvonne Ron...

Ron For what?

Yvonne Oh, stop it!

Ron Why didn't you tell me?

Yvonne What difference would it have made...

Ron Bloody hell...!

Yvonne Ron, it's nothing.

Ron Nothing.

Yvonne No.

Ron Nothing? I've got a wife who gets drunk and lets her head get stuck down the trousers of young men? What planet are you from?

Yvonne It was all part of it.

Ron So that makes it all right, then?

Yvonne It was just a bit of fun that went too far. All right, it went too far, that's all!

Ron That's all, that's all!

Yvonne Have you never done anything you feel guilty about?

Ron (*loudly*) You don't appear to feel guilty about it!

Yvonne Stop shouting.

Ron You'd go out and do it again tonight, you would!

Yvonne Stop it!

Ron Stop it? I'll kill you in a minute, good God I will!

Yvonne Oh, go on, then!

Ron I can't trust you, can I? I saw you one night kissing Peter after the *Showboat* party and that kiss lasted nearly a bloody hour!

Yvonne So what?

Ron I could swing for you, I could!

Yvonne Oh, go on, then!

Ron You're just not bothered, are you?

Yvonne No, I'm not and I'll tell you something else, it was the best night I've had in the last three years, if you must know.

Ron Ah ah!

Yvonne It was.

Ron I've heard you!

Yvonne It was the first time I've felt any excitement.

Ron slaps her across the face. Silence

Ron Sorry!

Yvonne Go on, little man. Hit me again. Go on, knock my teeth out! Slap me if that's what you want to do, slap me! (*She attacks Ron*)

Ron pathetically fights back

Ron Shut up! Shut up, for God's sake!

Yvonne Go on, make a complete fool of yourself...

Ron No, I'll leave you to do that, shall I?

Yvonne and Ron wrestle awkwardly as Grant comes from the caravan

Grant What's going on?

Ron Nothing.

Grant You all right?

Yvonne Yes.

Ron Everything's fine, go back to bed.
Grant Has he hit you?
Ron (*shouting*) I said go back to bed!
Grant Wow, steady, tha's not at school now! Are you all right?
Ron (*shouting*) Go back to bed!
Grant You shouldn't hit women. Didn't tha' learn that at college?
Ron She's all right...
Grant Ay, she looks it... Do you want to go inside with Steph while I have a word with Ron?
Ron Have a word? Have a word, you're the bloody reason she's like this...
Grant Go inside, love.
Yvonne Leave me, I'm all right.
Ron Leave her!

Yvonne is very emotional

Yvonne I'm sorry, Ron, Jesus Christ... I'm sorry ... but I felt so alive...
Ron Sorry?
Yvonne What can I say...?
Ron I ought to kill you, I did, honest...
Grant Hey, hey, now steady.
Ron Steady?
Grant Pack it in!
Ron Or what?
Grant You what?
Ron Or what? Come on, then! Come on! All my life I've been running from the likes of you! You're that bloody thick, it's frightening...
Grant Tha what?
Yvonne Ron, just leave it...

Ron picks up a HP sauce bottle and uses it as a weapon against Grant. He then uses it as a penis and pretends to pass wind through the next speech. It is pathetic

Ron I can be as crude as the rest, if that's what you're after, is it? Is it the animal you're after? Come on, let's get you sorted out...
Grant Go to bed, man, go to bed, you're not worth it... (*He turns*) And keep the fuckin' noise down, some of us are trying to have a bloody holiday! Good grief, some people just don't know how to fuckin' behave!

Grant exits

Ron stands still, Yvonne is prostrate and weeps. She grabs a can of beer

Yvonne Ron...?

Ron No, don't, don't ever speak to me again... (*He begins clearing away. He puts some rubbish into the waste bag and smells the rabbit giblets*)

Yvonne Ron?

Ron Have you put this rabbit in here?

Yvonne Eh?

Ron (*shouting*) It's theirs, isn't it? You ignorant pig...!

Yvonne What a bloody weekend...!

Ron What have they been playing at? Animal. Grunt! Arsehole!

A beat

Yvonne What mess... Gooor!

Ron I'll start to get cleared away, then. Jeeez...

Yvonne What can I say?

Ron (*almost in tears of desperation*) Look at that awning, that was a sodding waste of money and all, wasn't it? A soddin' wash out!

Yvonne begins to help Ron put the rubbish into a bin

Yvonne Ron?

Ron Don't...

Yvonne Ron...

Ron Don't say a word...

They both put the rubbish into bags. Music plays softly under. Silence. Then suddenly

Steph (*off*) Oh, oh, oh, Grant, oh, no, please, Grant, no, not that!

Ron Oh, we're off!

Yvonne Ron, please listen...

Ron Are you going to go in their caravan because you're not coming in here! (*He continues to put rubbish into the bag. He suddenly stops and looks at a piece of paper*) Well, look at that...!

Steph (*off*) Oh. Grant, oh, no, oh, oh, oh...

Yvonne What is it?

Ron The bloody instructions for the awning.

Steph (*off*) Oh, oh, oh, no...

Ron I can't bloody believe it... (*He goes to get the awning*)

Yvonne Leave that now...! For God's sake...

Ron I'll get it up now I've got these...

Yvonne Ron, it's midnight...

Steph (*off*) Oh, oh, oh, oh!

Ron starts to put the awning up. Yvonne sits and has a drink

Ron Just listen to that...
Yvonne Ron, leave it please...
Ron Just listen to 'em. Bloody animals. Just listen to that bloody noise...
Steph (*off*) Oh, oh, oh... Ah!!

A beat

Yvonne I know, isn't it wonderful?

Kool and the Gang, Ladies' Night *swells. Ron and Yvonne begin to put up their awning. They hold a piece of the awning structure, which is connected in four parts by wire. It is very floppy and difficult to control, it is a struggle for them to cope with, as——*

——the Lights fade to Black-out

FURNITURE AND PROPERTY LIST

Further dressing may be added at the director's discretion

Act I

Scene 1

On stage: Cut away half of new caravan, showing furniture and holiday
paraphernalia, with waste bin, gas bottle, lock on hitch, etc.

Personal: **Ron:** sun hat

Scene 2

On stage: As before

Scene 3

On stage: As before

Scene 4

Set: Tables
Chairs

Off stage: Large awning sack, metal pegs, hammer (**Ron**)

Scene 5

Set: Awning all out over pitch
Plastic boxes of food and cutlery

Scene 6

On stage: As before

Scene 7

Set: Picnic type food
              Bottle of wine
              Can of beer
              Small glass
              Script inside caravan

Scene 8

Set: Large old caravan with awning
              Can of beer
              Cassette player
              Tape cassette

Scene 9

Set: **Ron**'s and **Yvonne**'s bits and bobs

Personal: **Steph:** cigarettes, lighter (carried throughout)

Scene 10

Set: Remains of last night's snack
              Futurist Theatre leaflet in caravan

Off stage: 2 chairs (**Steph**)
              Newspaper (**Ron**)

Scene 11

On stage: **Yvonne** underwear on small washing line

Scene 12

Set: Small plastic table
                Can of beer

Scene 13

Set: Book

Scene 14

Set: Bottles
                Ron's pyjamas

Scene 15

Off stage: 2 rabbits (**Grant**)

Act II

Scene 1

Set: Gas bottle

Personal: **Ron:** handkerchief (carried throughout)

Scene 2

Set: Chair

Scene 3

Set: **Ron**'s and **Yvonne**'s chairs

Off stage: Large bowl of potato peelings (**Grant**)
                Empty cans of beans, carrier bag (**Steph**)

Scene 4

Set: **Grant**'s chair
             Can of beer

Scene 5

Set: Sandwiches

Scene 6

Off stage: Food remnants (**Steph**)
             Large cardboard crate of beer (**Grant**)

Scene 7

Set: Garden furniture

Scene 8

Set: Barbecue with large number of cheap party foods, empty cans of
                cheap beer, and still-glowing embers
             HP sauce bottle
             Ron's awning instructions

Off stage: Drinks (**SM**)
             Cans of beer (**Grant**)

LIGHTING PLOT

Property fittings required: torchlight
1 exterior. The same throughout

ACT I, Scene 1

To open: Scorching summer's day lighting

Cue 1   **Ron**: "Argh!"   (Page 1)
            Black-out

ACT I, Scene 2

To open: As before

Cue 2   **Ron**: "…is that any good?"   (Page 2)
            Black-out

ACT I, Scene 3

To open: As before

Cue 3   **Ron** exits   (Page 4)
            Black-out

ACT I, Scene 4

To open: As before

Cue 4   **Ron**: "Now is that the back or the front?"   (Page 6)
            Black-out

ACT I, Scene 5

To open: As before

Cue 5   **Yvonne**: "I'm unpacking."   (Page 6)
             Black-out

ACT I, Scene 6

To open: As before

Cue 6   **Ron**: "Yes, the story of my life."   (Page 7)
             Black-out

ACT I, Scene 7

To open: As before

Cue 7   **Ron**: "Not as good as she would've been."   (Page 9)
             Black-out

ACT I, Scene 8

To open: Evening lighting

Cue 8   **Ron**: "Oh, come on, this is ridiculous!"   (Page 14)
             Black-out

ACT I, Scene 9

To open: Evening lighting

Cue 9   **Ron**: "...for him to swing on."   (Page 17)
             Black-out

ACT I, Scene 10

To open: Summer morning lighting

Cue 10   **Ron** goes to change waste tank   (Page 22)
              Black-out

ACT I, SCENE 11

To open: Summer day's lighting

Cue 11   **Ron**: "I've done it!"   (Page 24)
              Black-out

ACT I, SCENE 12

To open: Evening lighting

Cue 12   **Ron** continues to put rubbish into plastic bag   (Page 30)
              Black-out

ACT I, SCENE 13

To open: Early evening lighting

ACT I, SCENE 14

To open: Combined night caravan site and Futurist Theatre lighting

Cue 13   Pop music swells   (Page 34)
              Fade lights to black

ACT I, SCENE 15

To open: Night lighting

Cue 14   **Steph** and **Yvonne** enter   (Page 34)
              Bring up torch lighting their way

Cue 15   Music plays   (Page 37)
              Fade lights to black-out

ACT II, Scene 1

To open: Very warm day lighting

Cue 16   **Ron**: "Yes, it does, doesn't it?"   (Page 41)
              Black-out

ACT II, Scene 2

To open: As before

Cue 17   **Ron**: "…I'll be getting this holiday!"   (Page 47)
              Black-out

ACT II, Scene 3

To open: Summer afternoon lighting

Cue 18   **Steph**: "You bloody idiot!"   (Page 50)
              Black-out

ACT II, Scene 4

To open: As before

Cue 19   **Yvonne** watches **Grant** exit   (Page 53)
              Black-out

ACT II, Scene 5

To open: Evening lighting, dim in caravan

Cue 20   **Ron**: "Yes, love, you tell me every day!"   (Page 57)
              Black-out

ACT II, Scene 6

To open: As before

82   Perfect Pitch

Cue 21   **Ron** goes back to awning   (Page 60)
            Black-out

ACT II, Scene 7

To open: As before

Cue 22   **Yvonne** smiles   (Page 62)
            Black-out

ACT II, Scene 8

To open: Night lighting

No cues

EFFECTS PLOT

ACT I

Cue 13	**Grant**: "No, I thought not!" *Birds twitter*	(Page 22)
Cue 14	**Ron** goes to change the waste tank *Music*	(Page 22)
Cue 15	**Ron** continues to put rubbish into plastic bag *Music*	(Page 30)
Cue 16	**Ron**: "No worries there, then?" *Farting sound effect in aid of* **Grant**	(Page 32)
Cue 17	**Ron** commences reading *Start sexy pop music and swell it up*	(Page 32)
Cue 18	To open Scene 14 *Continue sexy pop music*	(Page 33)
Cue 19	**Steph**: "...they haven't even started yet!" *Increase pop music*	(Page 34)
Cue 20	**Grant** switches on cassette player *Music: J S Bach's* Sheep May Safely Graze	(Page 34)
Cue 21	**Yvonne**: "Here, have a rabbit!" *Music plays*	(Page 37)

ACT II

Cue 22	**Ron**: "Yes, it does, doesn't it?" *Music*	(Page 41)
Cue 23	**Ron**: "...I'll be getting this holiday!" *Music*	(Page 47)
Cue 24	**Steph**: "You bloody idiot!" *Music*	(Page 50)
Cue 25	**Yvonne** watches **Grant** exit *Music*	(Page 53)
Cue 26	**Ron**: "Yes, love, you tell me every day!" *Music*	(Page 57)

Cue 27	**Ron** goes back to awning *Music*	(Page 60)
Cue 28	**Yvonne** smiles *Music*	(Page 62)
Cue 29	**Ron** and **Yvonne** put rubbish into bags *Play music softly under*	(Page 72)
Cue 30	**Yvonne**: "I know, isn't it wonderful?" *Music: Kool and the Gang's* Ladies Night	(Page 73)

MADE AND PRINTED IN GREAT BRITAIN BY
LATIMER TREND & COMPANY LTD PLYMOUTH
MADE IN ENGLAND

Lightning Source UK Ltd.
Milton Keynes UK
UKOW06f2338140717
305369UK00011B/220/P

9 780573 019661